GOD'S BUSINESS SCHOOL

Jewish Knowledge for Any Business

Joel S. Weiner

God's Business School
Jewish Knowledge for Any Business

First Edition, date of release 11/1/2024

Published by Enlightened Religion Press, LLC
Los Angeles, CA 90045
www.EnlightenedReligionPress.com

Paperback Edition:
ISBN-13: 979-8-9879502-7-2

E-book Format
ISBN-13: 979-8-9879502-8-9

Library of Congress Control Number: 2024918808

Cover design by: Larry Pobiner; Barbara Groves

DEDICATION

To philosophers:

We are civilized because of your profound insights.

To scientists:

We have learned so much about our universe from science. Your methods teach us how to explore nature's wonders.

To cultural innovators:

Your works make life interesting and fun.

To Jewish business leaders and professionals:

Your reputation for smart business makes us proud.

To my teachers:

You taught me how to learn. What a blessing.

To my rabbis:

You helped me appreciate life's greatest lessons.

I'm especially thankful to Rabbis Michael Shevack, Steven Fink, and Jack Bemporad, each of whom are friends who reviewed my manuscript and taught me along the way.

To my parents and their parents:

By your love and example, you showed me the way.

My sense of humor and street smarts start with you.

To Carol,

You are my partner in everything.

To my kids and grandkids,

It's all for you. Cherish your heritage. Learn from where I've left off.

GOD'S BUSINESS SCHOOL

Introduction

Pathway to success

Pay attention to this book! You will . . .

. . . enjoy your work more.

. . . be happier in your life.

. . . be more successful. Not just money, but more creative, more purposeful, more fulfilled.

. . . be energized; more motivated; more self-directed.

. . . be a better leader and manager.

. . . be more confident.

. . . make the world a better place.

Is this crazy? How could all this be true? Well, as you'll learn here, there is no sure thing. But learn the principles explained in this book; apply them yourself; and you will greatly improve your odds for success.

And, when something goes poorly, you'll be able to deal with it better. Realistically, everything does not go right the first time. Good businesspeople expect surprises.

Why am I so confident making these promises! Problems are complex, and it takes a multidisciplined approach to solve most problems.

Business is spiritual. Business problems are much better handled by integrating business know-how with "spirituality". This is not woo-woo stuff. There is foundational spiritual knowledge in Judaism that helps to . . .

. . . understand the real underlying causes of business problems.

. . . lead and motivate people to work together effectively.

. . . make work meaningful.

. . . build the business to succeed generation after generation.

There are plenty of books that teach business techniques and plenty of books on Judaism.

But there is precious little that puts it all together in a clear, practical, integrated way. This handbook does it.

Why Judaism?

Jews have a reputation for making money. We're good at this.

Jews are rightfully proud. Jewish expertise has built astonishingly successful businesses[1].

Jews were the founders of Wall Street giants like Goldman Sachs, Lehman Brothers, Salmon Brothers, Kuhn Loeb, Bache & Company.

In data sciences and communications, Jews started Google, Oracle, Dell, Facebook, and Comcast.

Food specialty companies like Starbucks, Ben & Jerry's, Dunkin' Donuts, Snapple, Haagen Dazs, and Slim Fast were all started by Jews.

In entertainment, Jews started Warner Brothers, Metro Goldwyn Mayer and DreamWorks.

In fashion, Calvin Klein, Ralph Lauren, Donna Karan, Estee Lauder, are all Jewish.

---

[1] Jews are less than 0.2% of the world's population. Yet, we Jews are more than 10% of the Forbes 400 wealthiest people. We Jews are more than 10% of the CEOs of the Fortune 500 largest corporations.

> Want to go shopping? Somewhere near you is a Jewish store: Kauffman's, Macy's, Filenes, Rich's, I. Magnin, Bloomingdales, Bergdorf Goodman, Nieman Marcus, Lazarus, Lane Bryant . . . Retail is in our genes. It's also in our jeans: *Levi Strauss.*

There are foundational principles taught in Judaism which when properly understood and exercised illumine a better way for life and business. Applied to business, these principles provide guidelines for determining which business solution provides the most good for the most people for the longest time. This leads to better, stronger businesses. In short, this builds more value.

These principles are not unique to Judaism. But Jewish experiences throughout the ages are unique, and through these experiences Jews have finely tuned these principles. Facing fierce anti-semitism Jews gravitated to the business fields that were open to them while building a culture that emphasized family values, education, hard work, and creativity. They developed skills in finance, trading, science, and medicine. They found support and solace in spirituality. They cultivated guidelines for business that reflected their spiritual studies. Jews also flourished in creative outlets such as music, writing, theatre and humor.

You'll find here a combination of Jewish principles and Jewish street-smarts that you can apply in your own business.

Anti-semitism

Anti-semitism is still a terrible scourge. Many Jews would say, "Shhh. Don't draw attention. We don't want to attract jealousy or worse." They fear anti-semitism, and rightfully so, because anti-semitism is on the rise.

Throughout history people have mistaken Jewish successes in business as somehow mysterious. What they don't understand, and what makes them jealous, antisemites turn into bias and hatred.

Also, there were a few criminals, like Boesky, Madoff, Milliken, and Epstein who amassed lots of money, but who went to prison. These guys did not follow *God*'s laws nor America's laws. In no way did they understand and practice this Jewish knowledge. They were scoundrels.

They are embarrassments to their families and to good Jews throughout the world.

Sharing this knowledge is intended to help everyone do better business. Also, please *God*, sharing this knowledge hopefully will help to fight anti-semitism.

There is much to be gained for everyone by understanding how much we have in common.

You don't have to be Jewish to get in on this.

Not all Jews are good businesspeople. That is a ridiculous stereotype.

And obviously there are plenty of Christians, Muslims and people of other religions who are good businesspeople.

Everyone can profit from the knowledge and lessons in this book!

After all, Jesus was born and schooled in Judaism. Christians who read further will recognize some of these principles, as they later formed the foundation of the *Protestant work ethic*[2]. They were well-known to

[2] Max Weber; Peter R. Baehr; Gordon C. Wells, The Protestant Ethic and the "Spirit" of Capitalism, Penguin Twentieth Century Classics, April 1, 2002

Emerson, Franklin, and Jefferson.

Muslims, too, will recognize similarities.

Christianity, Islam and Judaism have the same father, Abraham. We'll delve into and learn from Abraham's story. He is pivotal. Abraham had keen observational skills, much like a scientist. And he built his family's business by committing to a vision, much like an entrepreneur. Abraham's insights and visionary behavior happened long before the words "scientist" and "entrepreneur" were even invented.

This book goes through all aspects of running a business and provides examples of foundational knowledge discovered by the early Hebrews. Included also are contemporary quotes, stories, and descriptions of businesses to illustrate how these key principles are applicable to contemporary business situations.

But I'm not selling a religion here. Jewish knowledge is applicable and can be interpreted for other traditions. I wholeheartedly share this know-how for everyone. The lessons in this book are universal, practical, and tried and true. Everyone's business can be improved. This book can pay off for everyone. Success follows.

Take that to the bank!

Part 1: Freshman Orientation

History of Jews in Business

Jewish success in business has been nourished by . . .

. . . experiences running small businesses.

. . . strong family ties.

. . . hard work discipline.

. . . serving as finance advisors and intermediaries.

. . . connecting to *God.*

Jewish economic history goes back at least to 2000 BCE[3]. The ancient Hebrews were farmers, craftsmen, and traders. Farming and hunting, of course, are the oldest occupations. People need to eat. Additionally, archeologists have uncovered evidence that people in that time and place lived in villages and towns. They were good at glass production, pottery, and distilling barley to produce beer. They exported many goods including clothing, carpets, tools, weapons and jewelry[4] to Syria and Egypt

Unfortunately, that land was continually a target for conquerors, largely because of its location on key trading crossroads. The Jews were cast out of that land numerous times throughout history.

Nebuchadnezzar, a Babylonian king, conquered the land and destroyed the *First Temple* which had been constructed by Solomon. The Jews were deported from *Judah* (what is now Israel) to Babylonia in 590-580 BCE. Jews returned to Jerusalem in several waves afterwards, although many Jews remained throughout Mesopotamia.

Nevertheless, the Jews excellence in the trades continued. At the time of

---

[3] Jews use the nomenclature BCE ("Before the Common Era") rather than BC ("Before Christ"). Similarly, Jews use CE ("Common Era") rather than AD ("Anno Domini") when referring to years after Jesus' birth.
[4] Chaim Potok, Wanderings, Alfred A. Knopf, New York 1978

Hillel (first century BCE) and Jesus (first century CE) Jews were farmers, hunters and fishermen. They also were stonecutters, carpenters, tailors, smiths, weavers, potters and glass smelters.[5]

The Romans destroyed the *Second Temple* in Jerusalem in 70 CE. This was another watershed event. Jewish scholars settled in what is now Northern Israel and redefined how Judaism was to be practiced. No longer was the emphasis on animal sacrifice in the *Holy Temple*. The rabbinic age began with an emphasis on synagogue prayer and religious practices.

Throughout the Middle Ages Jews suffered outright discrimination. They resided in countries throughout most of the world, but generally were not permitted to own land, participate in government, or join professional guilds. They had to rely on small, family owned and operated businesses.

Literacy among Jews was relatively high. This was partly because Jews who were not educated in Jewish texts tended to convert to the dominant religions in whatever country they resided[6].

Jews also were well-suited for trading and banking since they were represented in many countries and shared a common language.

Americans recognize 1492 as the year that Columbus discovered America. 1492 also was the year that Jews were deported from Spain as part of the *Spanish Inquisition*. Prior to 1492 there was a well-established Jewish community, *Sephardic Jews*, throughout Spain.

In the sixteenth century a few notable events occurred.

> Mayer Rothschild expanded his banking business by establishing each of his sons in offices throughout Europe.

---

[5] Ibid

[6] Maristella Botticini and Zvi Eckstein, The Chosen Few: How Education Shaped Jewish History, 70-1492, Princeton, 2012

Chasidism emerged under the guidance of the *Baal Shem Tov*[7]. Jews who were not formerly schooled were taught to connect directly and spiritually with *God* through dancing and singing that energized their prayer practices.

Napoleon granted Jews citizenship of France, the first time that Jews were permitted this right anywhere in Europe.

Despite these generally positive events, antisemitism still occurred in cycles. Jewish culture persevered as it had done throughout time. Jewish economic life was heavily focused on trades and trading. Jewish small businesses survived because they had to.

The most outrageous and terrible persecution was perpetrated by the Nazis in World War II. Nazi persecution of Jews escalated in the decade leading up to WWII, and during WWII approximately 6 million Jews were murdered by the Nazis. Entire populations of Jews in towns across most of Europe were slaughtered.

In the aftermath of WWII, the modern State of Israel was reborn. Israel had to fight for its survival in several wars, including its "War for Independence" in 1948 and to push back invasion by neighboring Arab countries in 1967 ("Six Day War") and 1973 ("*Yom Kippur* War"). Violence on Israel's borders has been continual. On October 7, 2023, Hamas invaded southern Israel torturing and killing many non-combatant Israelis and taking hundreds of Israelis hostage.

Both Israel's miliary and economy are highly admired. Israeli technology has made significant advances in agriculture, communications and encryption, medicine and pharmacology, energy, defense and other fields.

In America Jews gravitated to those businesses that permitted them access and afforded entrepreneurial opportunities.

Jews became physicians, dentists, attorneys, and accountants since

---

[7] Israel ben Eliezer (1698-1760) was known as *Baal Shem Tov*, Hebrew for "Master of the Good Name".

advancement in those fields are based primarily on education. Professionals could succeed as individual proprietors or as small partnerships.

Jewish immigrants arrived in New York in the 1800's and earned fortunes in banking[8]. For example, Goldman Sachs continues today as a premier investment banking firm. Kuhn, Loeb & Co. was founded in 1867 by Abraham Kuhn and Solomon Loeb and grew to prominence under the leadership of Jacob Schiff, Loeb's son-in-law. That firm merged with Lehman Brothers in 1977 and was acquired by American Express in 1984.

Hollywood's major studios were mostly founded in the early 20th century by Jews who immigrated to the United States from Eastern Europe. There were few social barriers in Hollywood, and cinema grew out of vaudeville where Jews had already found a toehold. Carl Laemmle (Universal), Adolph Zukor (Paramount), William Fox (Fox), Louis B. Mayer (MGM), and Benjamin Warner (Warner) were all Jewish silver-screen pioneers.[9]

---

[8] Daniel Schulman, The Money Kings, Knopf, 2023

[9] Neal Gabler, An Empire of Their Own: How the Jews Invented Hollywood, Random House, 1998

The God Question

It's difficult to discuss *God* with others, because so many of us have different ideas of "*God*".

God and Nature

Let's start with some observable facts.

> Our universe exists. Rabbi Richard Simon, a teacher and friend of mine, is fond of saying, "If I punch you in the nose will it hurt? Of course it would. You exist." Look around. We live in the world. It exists. How did it get here?
>
> We don't know what existed before our universe was created. We cannot peer back in time before the "Big Bang" and may never be able to do so. Scientific hypotheses of what came before are just that, "hypotheses". Not observable.
>
> We don't know what lays beyond our universe. Our universe is vast and is expanding at ever increasing speed. In the future some stars will be so far from earth that light from those stars will never reach earth. Thus, what lies beyond is a mystery for which we may never be able to discover answers.
>
> Nature has many mysteries that we don't understand. For example, our universe is comprised of "dark matter" and "dark energy" that we cannot "see", and this stuff makes up most of what is in outer space.

Ancient humans invented the notion of gods to explain nature's mysteries that they could not explain.

Judaism's #1 contribution is the idea that there must be one *God* above all other gods. We trace this insight back to Abraham. Jews consider *God* to be the ultimate Creator.

God and Good

Jews revere *God* above all else and view *Torah*[10] as a foundational text. *Genesis,* the first book of *Torah,* introduces key lessons about knowledge, good and evil, and the value all Life and Creation. These are lessons for life and, by extension, for every business.

Genesis also teaches us the story of *Abraham. God* commanded Abraham to "Go forth to a land that I will show you". And "I will make of you a great nation." Abraham's life took on meaningful purpose. You can see the relevance here for any business. A common purpose is a great motivator.

Torah goes on in *Exodus*. We meet *Moses*. The Hebrews[11] receive the *Ten Commandments* from *God.* A code of good conduct begins to develop. This code of conduct is further developed later in *Torah* and other Jewish texts.

Thomas Cahill[12] wrote that Jews view a person's lifetime as a journey holding the possibility of a better tomorrow. Jews use the term *Tikkun Olam,* meaning "repair the world", to describe our life's purpose. We want to leave the world better for our children and their children.

> *You shall love your neighbor as yourself.*
>
> \- *Leviticus* 19:18

> *The stranger who sojourns with you shall be to you as the native among you, and you shall love him as yourself; for you were strangers in the land of Egypt.*
>
> \- *Leviticus* 19:34

These verses from *Leviticus* exemplify how we should deal with other people, whether they are neighbors or strangers. Christians will recognize *Leviticus* 19:18, since Jesus taught this same message, and it became known as the "Golden Rule".

---

[10] See subsequent section describing "Torah".
[11] The Hebrews were not referred to as Jews until later.
[12] Thomas Cahill, The Gifts of the Jews, Anchor, 1999

"Treat every customer as you would want to be treated yourself".

I call this the "business golden rule". That is how you build a great business.

If you take away anything from this book it is this: "being good" is what builds value. Focusing on "being good" leads to riches. True wisdom comes from discerning what is good and adopting practices in your life, including in your business dealings, that are good.

Therefore, whether or not you believe in *God*, at least think of the word "*God*" as a contraction for the word "Good".

Personal Reflections

I see no disconnect between science and Judaism. The following story illustrates where I'm coming from.

> A new rabbi had started at my synagogue, and after she had led her first *Shabbat* (Sabbath) evening service I spoke with her.
>
> I pointed out, "Rabbi, nice service. But I noticed that you didn't mention *God* at all throughout the service."
>
> She responded, "I don't mention *God*, because a lot of people have trouble saying "*God*" directly."
>
> Wow! Epiphany. I told her, "Rabbi, if you have trouble mentioning *God* out loud then we really have a problem."

Unfortunately, the above true story is not unusual. Like many, I was uncomfortable with the idea of *God* for most of my life.

I think my experience was similar to many Jewish kids in the latter half of the 20th Century. My parents wanted me to have a good Jewish education, and at the same time enjoy the advantages of a public-school secular education.

In religious school there was seldom talk of science. And, in public school there was essentially no talk about *God*. There was separation of church and state, both ways.

This separation of church and state is a good thing. We wouldn't want it any other way. It's necessary for a pluralistic democracy.

But it is confusing, especially for a child.

I was inclined towards science. I have always been fascinated by astronomy, chemistry and biology. It's all about nature.

When I couldn't rationalize the children's Bible stories my reaction was to reject them.

Years later I appreciated Bible stories could be interpreted as remembered history as well as fables and poetic stories that were very meaningful to my ancestors.

Orthodox Jews and others may regard *Torah* literally as the word of *God*. That is okay. I don't mean to offend anybody. We're all studying and learning valuable lessons from the same text.

I began to appreciate three things about *Torah:*

> *Torah* stories reflect keen observation of nature, just as are scientific findings.
>
> *Torah* stories illustrate moral truths.
>
> Knowledge comes both from science and religious traditions. Both viewpoints benefit by appreciating the other. Focusing on differences misses the point.

For example, Newton's Laws of Gravity were brilliant observations about nature that were very valuable. Years later, Einstein showed that Newton's equations were approximations. In other words, Newton's so-called "Laws" were not universally true. Not a surprise. Newton's discoveries were in the 17th century. Einstein's discoveries were made about 300 years later.

So, should we be surprised that observations about nature that were written down in *Torah* thousands of years ago were not exact explanations about nature? Of course not. If we can marvel at Newton's discoveries which are about 300 years old, we surely should marvel at Abraham's discoveries which were over 3000 years old. Newton's Laws, by the way, still work extremely well to solve many physics problems.

Now, back to the story about the young rabbi at my synagogue. I had become the president of that synagogue in large part because I had a strong business background, and that synagogue was in financial trouble. As part of that experience, I saw first-hand the difficulties of running a non-profit enterprise without good business processes. And I saw the disaffection of many adults with “religion”.

People want their synagogue, first and foremost, to provide a welcoming feeling of community. Adults also want their synagogue to provide “Yiddishkeit” (a feeling of tradition) as well as Jewish learning that is stimulating, meaningful, and relevant. Each of these attributes, feeling Judaism and understanding Judaism, are desired in different proportions depending upon individual. My perception is that many contemporary synagogues don’t emphasize understanding Judaism enough.

Instinctively or because my parents were good people, I was always a good student, a well-meaning person, and a good worker. Judaism and family examples always guided my behavior. But I didn’t understand enough *Torah* to verbalize “why” nor to incorporate Jewish knowledge to make what I knew about business practices be even more effective.

Beshert, fate, while I was a synagogue president I started to learn *Torah* with a teacher, a rabbi, who appreciated my mathematical and business training. We learned together, and we became good friends in the process. I am still learning.

When I read *Torah,* now open-mindedly, I see how relevant its wisdom is. I truly marvel at the synchronicity of the insights in *Torah* and science. And I also understand better how good business practices are so consistent with good Jewish practices.

I have no regrets, but it would have been wonderful to have had this book early in my career. Understanding business best practices harmoniously alongside the context of Judaic knowledge would have been very powerful. It would have provided me more confidence and made me even more effective.

The longer a blind man lives, the more he sees.

-*Yiddish* Saying

Now, back to the story about the young rabbi at my synagogue. I had

Torah, Talmud, Midrash

This book illustrates how Jewish wisdom applies to contemporary business situations. Brief quotes from *Torah*, *Talmud*, and other Jewish sources highlight these lessons.

Torah is often called the "Five Books of Moses". It is the sacred text of Judaism.

The Hebrew bible, *Tanakh*, includes *Torah*, *Nevi'im* ("Prophets"), and *Ketuvim* ("Writings"). Christians refer to this as the "Old Testament".

Talmud is a collection of writings that covers Jewish law and tradition, compiled and edited between the third and sixth centuries. There is a Jerusalem Talmud (circa 400 BCE) and a Babylonian Talmud (circa 600 BCE). The quotes in this book are from the Babylonian Talmud.

Midrash is commentary that refers to a passage in *Torah* meant to explain, illustrate or expand on that passage. *Talmud* includes *midrash*, but *midrashim* also were written later by various rabbis including to the present day. Consequently, available commentary on *Torah* is vast. Some *midrashim* have been repeated so often that they have become famous teachings in themselves.

Yiddish is a West Germanic language spoken by *Ashkenazi* Jews and traditionally written utilizing the Hebrew alphabet. *Yiddish* originated in 9th century Europe and reached its peak prior to WWII. Many *Yiddish* expressions reflect ancient Jewish insights mixed with sarcasm and streetwise wit.

"Torah" also is utilized sometimes in context to refer broadly to Judaic wisdom from *Tanakh*, *Talmud* or other Jewish texts.

The *Tanakh* was written in Hebrew. Quotes included here are from the Revised Standard English translation published in 1952 by the National Council of Churches of Christ in the USA. This translation was influenced by the Dead Sea Scrolls and the Septuagint, which itself was a translation into Greek completed by Jewish scholars. Other English translations may vary. I've utilized this English translation to be especially open and welcoming to the widest audience.

Jews refer to the books of *Torah* by the first word in that book, and so the first book of *Torah* is traditionally referred to as *Bereisheit*, which is Hebrew and translates to English as "In the beginning". The title *Genesis* is the title of the same book in Greek. The Greek titles of the books in *Torah* are referenced in this book for familiarity for all.

Part 2 - Foundational Knowledge

Genesis of Value

In the beginning God created the heaven and the earth.

- *Genesis* 1:1

Judaism's fundamental and greatest insight is the understanding that there must be one *God* above all else. "*God*" is the "*Creator.*"

God gave us the gift of intelligence.

> *Then God said, "Let us make man in our image, after our likeness.*

- *Genesis* 1:26

What does it mean that we are "created in the image of *God*". We don't know what *God* looks like. *God*'s infiniteness cannot be rendered as an image.

God gave us the gift of intelligence. Our ability to think and create are *God*-like qualities. That is what Jews mean by being created in the image of *God*.

And God saw everything that he had made and, behold, found it very good.

- *Genesis* 1:31

The Hebrew for "good" *is "tov"* which implies "complete"; "connected"; "in harmony with". Thus, Creation is a process. It is continuing.

God is the *Creator*. We are co-creators. We endeavor to be *God*-like by creating add-ons to Creation that make sense. That is what we mean by doing good.

Who's the Boss?

Torah's description of the creation of the universe is uncannily similar to how contemporary astrophysicists understand its inception. Quibbling about the differences is silly. Marveling at the amazing similarities is spiritually up-lifting.

Does the universe exist? Of course, it does.

We observe the existence of the universe. We live in the universe, along with an uncountable number of other species of life. We see, smell, hear, and touch things around us. All of it, our perceptions of it and the things themselves, are miracles.

We've come to understand that all life is connected. Each species has adapted to its own niche in the environment, and the overall environment is impacted by what happens in each niche.

Everything is *connected.*

Our Sun is one of billions of other stars in the universe. Stars are born (created) and die (explode or collapse) in time, although the lifetime of stars is so very long that it's almost beyond our comprehension.

Carl Sagan[13] said, "We are all made of stardust". Everything on Earth came from elements that originated from exploding stars in our universe. Sagan was trying to explain how we should be humble and appreciate the connections between us.

The universe is *infinite*.

Astrophysicists have discovered that the universe began about 14 billion years ago in what has come to be known as the "Big Bang", and the universe is still expanding. We do not know, and may never know, what is beyond the universe or what came before the universe.

Most of what astrophysicists have learned about the beginnings of our universe is less than 100 years old.

Humans create every day. Each day is a new beginning. We can choose our own actions, and doing so we can shape our own future. There are

---

[13] Carl Sagan (1934 - 1996) was a famous astrophysicist, author, and teacher. Sagan grew up as a Reform Jew in Brooklyn.

infinite possibilities for our actions. This is *freedom.*

Intelligence and freedom go hand-in-hand, and freedom implies responsibility. We can choose to create a better future.

This is the Jewish view of Reality, which is closely linked to our awe of Creation and the Creator, *God.*

Everyone can observe Creation and its awesomeness. No religion is needed.

Jews, among various denominations, have different ideas about *God*, and that is okay[14]. Whatever else you believe, or don't believe, about *God*, for our purposes in this book it is only necessary that when you say "*God*" you are referring to the Creator.

God is the original entrepreneur, and everything is *God*'s enterprise. Everything that we have or will have is a gift from *God.*

Knowledge - Do Good

The *Garden of Eden* was perfect. It was magical, care-free, beautiful, and abundant. It also was impossible. To put it differently, life as we know it would not be if we were still in the *Garden of Eden.*

> *And the Lord God commanded the man, saying, "You may eat freely of every tree of the garden, but the tree of knowledge of good and evil you shall not eat, for in the day that you eat of it you shall die.*
>
> \- *Genesis* 2:16-17

Adam and Eve were not fully aware of themselves or what they were doing. They were like babies. Like babies, Adam and Eve hadn't yet learned that in the world there is both good and bad. Initially, *God* protected Adam and Eve, not wanting or at least delaying them from learning about good and bad.

---

[14] Christians, too, have different ideas about *God.*

> *But the serpent said to the woman, "You will not die, for God knows that when you eat of it your eyes will be opened and you will be like God knowing good and evil.*
>
> \- *Genesis* 3:4-5

Eve could not resist eating the fruit of the tree, from the Tree of Knowledge. Her desire for knowledge was overwhelming.

> *So when the woman saw that the tree was good for food and that it was a delight to the eyes, and that the tree was to be desired to make one wise, she took of its fruit and ate, and she also gave some to her husband*[15]*, and he ate.*
>
> \- *Genesis* 3-5-6

Eve found *knowledge,* and she gave that gift to Adam.

Intelligence, as precious a gift as it is, comes with burdens. Adam and Eve were not innocent anymore.

This is the story of every human baby. They open their eyes, literally and figuratively, and begin to see the world as it is.

Like a baby being forced out of the womb, Adam and Eve's experience in the *Garden of Eden* was ended[16]. They had to learn and decide for themselves what was "good". They had to learn that there are negative consequences, what they do "bad".

"Good" versus "Bad"? We see that the world contains good and bad. Since *God* created the world, Jews conclude that the dichotomy of good versus bad has a purpose.

God gave humans the gift of intelligence, so that humans could judge the

---

[15] That Adam was tempted by Eve to eat the apple also is an important part of the story. Sex is a very important motivator, and it is utilized very often in business advertising.

[16] Some people take this bible story literally. Others understand Eden to be a metaphor, a protected place where the inhabitants are naive about the evil around them.

differences between good and bad.

Humans can conceptualize the future. We can think ahead and anticipate the consequences of our actions. That is "free will".

Doing good is our purpose. We are to be partners with *God* in the ongoing perfection of the world. Judaism calls this *Tikkun Olam,* which is Hebrew for "Repair the World".

Free will is fundamental for business, as it is in life. Customers are free to choose what they want and what they perceive is worth buying. Businesses are forever trying to anticipate what customers want and bring those goods and services to market.

The purpose for us as individuals is to do Good.

The purpose of a business is to generate Value.

What is Good should be Valuable.

Many businesses compete based on price: "Our prices cannot be beat!" "We'll match any price!" This is a surefire way to have lower profit margins. Perhaps a business can make it up in volume, but not over the long haul.

Very successful businesses, and businesses that perform well over the long term, compete by being "good". *Ben & Jerry's Ice Cream* really tastes great and comes in a range of unique flavors. *Goldman Sachs* has the expertise to handle large scale financial transactions, and consequently is a go-to choice for large companies requiring investment banking services. *Bloomingdale's* perennially can be counted on to have the latest styles, eye-catching merchandise displays, and a wide range of fashion choices.

How a business produces products that are good and influences customers to perceive its products as good requires creativity, that *God*-like characteristic. This is what makes business so fascinating.

Be a Steward of All Life and Creation

> *Then God said, "Let us make man in our image, after our likeness; and let them have dominion over the fish of the sea, and over the birds of the air, and over the cattle, and over all the earth, and over every creeping thing that creeps upon the earth."*
>
> - *Genesis* 1:26

God has given us the gift to be able to create. After all, "*we are made in the image and likeness of God*". But we must humbly acknowledge that we are not *"The" Creator*. We are only "*a" creator*.

We now know that the earth is revolving around our sun; our sun moves around the Milky Way; and our entire galaxy moves through space. We are all fellow travelers through space.

To the extent that humans can control things on earth, we must remember that we are but caretakers of a small portion of *God*'s Creation.

Ecology was recognized as a field of science beginning in the 1890's. *Torah* anticipated the connectedness of all life and the importance of caring for all life thousands of years earlier.

The story of Noah illustrates our obligation to care for all life.

> *And of every living thing of all flesh, you shall bring two of every sort into the ark, to keep them alive with you; they shall be male and female.*
>
> - *Genesis* 6:19

Noah, his family, and all of life drifted on the waters when the floods came. From this story we learn that caring for all of life is the only road to survival.

From the Jewish point of view, humans have the privilege of having *dominion* over the earth and life on earth. But *dominion* is not *domination*! We are stewards, caretakers, with regards to nature. *God* gave us the gift of intelligence, so that we can impact upon nature, but naturally (pun intended) our obligation is to do so intelligently. We respect that *God* is the Creator - not us.

> *A Psalm of David. The earth is the Lord's and the fulness thereof, the world and those who dwell therein; for he has founded it upon the seas, and established it upon the rivers. Who shall ascend the hill of the Lord?*
> *And who shall stand in his holy place?*
> *He who has clean hands and a pure heart, who does not lift up his soul to what is false, and does not swear deceitfully. He will receive blessing from the Lord, and vindication from the God of his salvation.*
>
> - Psalms 24, 1-5

When you don't have "clean hands and a pure heart", our *dominion* becomes morally infected with *domination*. Understanding the distinction between *dominion* and *domination* takes intelligence and spiritual awareness. How we exercise our *dominion* so as not to *dominate* other species can be a matter of degree.

> We have the ability to plan our actions over long periods of time.
>
> We have the capability to learn about how other life forms interrelate to each other.
>
> We can communicate over long distances and pass knowledge to future generations utilizing sophisticated tools.
>
> We can think spiritually and have developed ethical and moral[17] codes of conduct.

Consequently, we are stewards of all Life and Creation. We must protect other species and natural resources. This is both our gift and our

---

[17] "Ethics" and "morality" are often used interchangeably. "Ethics" tends to refer to social rules, right versus wrong behaviors amongst the community. "Morals" tends to refer to right versus wrong behaviors for an individual.

responsibility.

When we create, it is inevitable (Physicists would tell us, "It is necessary.") that we also use energy, which comes from natural resources. Nothing is free. Yielding outputs requires utilizing inputs. In addition, since no process is perfect, there are always by-products.

Each of us as individuals has a role here, and more and more individuals are learning to consider these kinds of tradeoffs thoughtfully.

But in a big way, these tradeoffs are decided in the executive suites of large businesses, and it is difficult for a business to balance the costs versus benefits in other than money terms.

So, this Jewish spiritual lesson applies to the capitalist as well as the environmentalist.

God's purpose first. Human profit second.

And if you will obey my commandments which I command you this day, to love the Lord your God, and to serve him with all your heart and with all your soul, he will give the rain for your land in its season, the early rain and the later rain, that you may gather in your grain and your wine and your oil.

\- *Deuteronomy* 11:13-14

Be Kind to Others

> *You shall not take vengeance or bear any grudge against the sons of your own people, but you shall love your neighbor as yourself: I am the Lord.*

\- *Leviticus* 19:18

The translation of this verse from the original Hebrew more closely says, "Love your fellow human being because he is fundamentally equal to you."[18] The important implication is that we must be kind to everyone, not just people closely associated with ourselves.

In one form or another this rule is taught to children in synagogues and churches everywhere.

> Hillel, a famous teacher who lived in the first century BCE, was asked to explain *Torah*. Hillel responded, "That which is hateful to you, do not do unto your fellow. That is the whole *Torah*; the rest is commentary; now go and learn."
>
> And about 100 years after Hillel, Jesus taught "You shall love your neighbor". (*Matthew* 7:12). Jesus' wording came to be known as the "Golden Rule".

This is more than commonsense. We learned in the last chapter to "Be a steward of all Life and Creation." Creation includes humans. Duh! Every person is created in the image of *God*, and so every person has potential to be holy.

> *Say to all the congregation of the people of Israel, you shall be holy; for I the Lord your God am holy.*
>
> \- *Leviticus* 19:2

But it is so easy to forget this as we go about our busy lives. Treating each person that we encounter with respect and kindness honors Creation; it is a blessing to *God*. And not being respectful and kind to another person is a blasphemy to *God*.

Imagine how much better the world would be if more people truly acted towards other people with the knowledge that each person is holy. Imagine how much happier you would be engaging with other people, including strangers, if you reminded yourself of the other person's holiness. Not only would you be happier, so would the other person.

Do this, and you will be amazed at the results. You will be more successful in life, and in business.

---

[18] Rabbi Jack Bemporad, personal communication

Every business transaction has a seller and a buyer. Both sides, seller and buyer, should leave happier than they were before the transaction. Both sides have obligations to each other as we'll see throughout these lessons. Jewish business rules are all about treating the other person as they, themselves, would like to be treated.

This "business golden rule" goes for customers, employees, bosses, investors, suppliers and distributors — everyone.

> *Treat all your customers as you would want to be treated.*
>
> *Treat everyone involved with your business as you would want to be treated.*

Put It To Work

Asah (Hebrew meaning "Do"):

- Respect all people, all life and all creation! Everyone has potential.
- Say a prayer of thanks. Appreciate that the food you eat, the clothes you wear, the house you live in comes initially from nature. Thank *God* for the gifts from nature, for the gift of technology, and the ability to develop these gifts from nature into the myriads of things that make our lives better.
- Don't waste resources.
- Remember this "business golden rule".
  - Make your customers happy. Treat your customers as you would like to be treated.
  - Treat your colleagues, partners, investors as you would like to be treated.
- Uncover disagreements; they are not always out in the open. Probe to make sure that your customers are satisfied. Don't assume that others

agree with you, just because they are silent.

Bara (Hebrew meaning "Create"):

- Be open minded about your sources of knowledge. Science and spirituality, for example, are different paths to a fuller understanding of life. So, too, are music and art different pathways to gain insight.

- Read history, including the Bible. Keep in mind that previous generations had different levels of exposure to all the fields of knowledge, and so people throughout history saw their experiences through a different lens. Understand this and history will be more relevant to your own, present-day experiences.

- Starting and running a business takes creativity and knowledge. Be mindful that your creativity and ability to learn are gifts from *God*. Use your gifts wisely. That is how you thank the Giver!

- Be both audacious and humble! Audacious: you are creating something from nothing. Humble: You are part of something much bigger than yourself.

- Leverage your knowledge to do Good in the world.

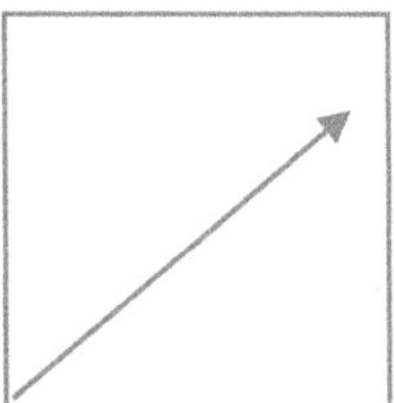

Be Creative, Like God

And God said, "Let there be light", and there was light.

- *Genesis* 1:3

Awesome! *God*'s creation of light was a momentous start to our universe.

"Light" is an important spiritual symbol in Judaism. Light connotes goodness and wisdom. Jewish ritual candles are lit at the start of Jewish holidays. Light reminds us of the Divine presence, making these events special and holy.

We now know that light is fundamental in our universe. Everything that exists comes from the energy that is light.

We also understand that humans only see a small portion of light. We call this "visible light". While some animals see light that is outside the spectrum visible to humans, there are frequencies of light beyond what any animal can see.

Also, our universe contains "dark matter' and "dark energy" which are recent discoveries and which we hardly understand. Yet, *God* created all of this. *God* is beyond our human abilities to fully understand.

Human creativity is not close to the awesomeness of *God*'s Creation. Yet, each of us creates. We create in different ways. Some human creations seem awesome. We also do good deeds every day, many times on a small scale and unseen by others. That is being creative, too.

When we think and do good things, big or small, it is awesome!

Be An Entrepreneur

The world always seems brighter when you've just made something that wasn't there before.

- Neil Gaiman[19]

An entrepreneur intentionally creates something new through their work. Entrepreneurial creativity occurs on many levels.

Obviously, if you run your own business, you are an entrepreneur.

But what if you run a department? Managing your department is like managing your own business in many ways. You have suppliers and customers, and you must satisfy your customers. Your department must add value.

The same goes if you manage a process within a department.

The key is to think like an entrepreneur. Think like an owner of the business, or the portion of the business that you manage. Be a leader. Have the passion to develop something new, something better. Set a path and take accountability to achieve results.

Everyone in business, no matter your position or your years of experience, should consider themselves to be an entrepreneur. Even the new beginning employee who is just starting their career no doubt aspires to advance. Every employee should learn and develop their skills as an entrepreneur by understanding and contributing to the overall goals of their work team.

Being an entrepreneur is hard work, but it also is fun and rewarding. You get tremendous *naches*[20] (pleasure) when your business makes progress towards fulfilling your vision.

Many things go into achieving business success. It's a process. It starts with your vision, an idea. Then, usually you develop a business plan, which is an organized way to outline all the necessary resources and key

---

[19] Gaiman is a popular contemporary author. He is most famous for the "Sandman" comic book series. Gaiman is Jewish. His great-grandfather emigrated from Belgium to the UK before 1914.

[20] "Naches" (*Yiddish*) is the pride and feelings of joy that you get from accomplishing something, or especially when your child accomplishes something good.

steps that your business would need to accomplish.

Business planning is not meant to be a once-and-done exercise. As you run your business you will encounter unexpected occurrences, obstacles as well as opportunities. You will need to attract and motivate people with the requisite skills and experience that your business needs. You will have customers, and you will learn to adapt to please your customers changing requirements.

Pause for a moment and consider what work is like if you don't approach your work like an entrepreneur. Some workers put in their time at work and do what is demanded of them. They collect their paycheck transactionally. They sell their time for dollars. That is not entrepreneurial.

Jewish knowledge sanctifies work as a holy endeavor to do good in the world. Business becomes a means to get more done with a team of like-minded people. Business becomes creative.

Jewish knowledge provides both spiritual and practical advice for all aspects of your business. You'll also find that this knowledge becomes self-reinforcing. As with anything worth learning, you'll get better at it with practice. For example, my wife and I have found the examples in this book to be relevant as we've discussed politics, social situations and teaching experiences with our grandchildren. I notice applicability to investing and other business situations that I've encountered recently. When you put this knowledge into practice it makes more and more sense, and it becomes easier.

You'll become wiser. You will become your own business coach.

Your Vision

Your first step, your "ah-hah" moment is the spark of your imagination. This is your business vision. This begins the process of making your dream real.

Think big! Let your imagination run. What is your idea, and how much good would your idea achieve? When you dream of the future for your business what does success look like?

Don't dwell on the difficulties yet. Naturally, you'll deal with difficulties and other limitations later. But, in the beginning there is only light.

Different people create differently. Different styles. Artists paint, musicians play, writers write, inventors invent, and scientists experiment. Whatever your talents are, leverage them.

Notice that even the greatest artists practice, try out their ideas. Rembrandt[21], for example, did small studies, sketches, before paint went onto canvas. Most of the great art masters worked this way, sometimes working on smaller studies for a year or more before putting their creation on a big canvas. Lesson: big ideas may take several steps and lots of time to come to fruition.

Most people have a favorite time of the day to do their thinking. There are morning people and late-night people.

Solve problems. When a new gadget that seems useful is introduced, do you sometimes slap your head and say to yourself, "Why didn't I think of that?" Try to notice things in your everyday life that could be a little bit better. Sometimes a "little bit better" leads to the genesis of a very good, creative idea.

Think outside the box. Search for the underlying assumptions that people seem to make. What if that assumption could be different? Would that make a big difference? Maybe trying another way, with a new assumption, would be a breakthrough.

> The Space Shuttle Columbia crashed shortly after launch in what was one of the biggest disasters in U.S. space exploration. The Space Shuttle Endeavor was a successor to Columbia, and Endeavor had successful missions until it was finally decommissioned in 2011. However, on one of the earlier Space Shuttle Endeavor flights some heat tiles fell off during launch, and NASA engineers were very worried about the shuttle's ability to withstand the heat from friction when the shuttle landed, descending rapidly through the earth's atmosphere.
>
> At the time I said to my co-workers, as we were watching the Endeavor's re-entry on television during our lunch break that a better solution was needed. I said, "Why don't they just come in slower, so that there wouldn't be so much friction?" This got a laugh. It was so

[21] Rembrandt, the great 17th Century Dutch master painter, was not Jewish, but he is known for paintings of Jews and scenes from Hebrew scripture.

obvious, and yet seemingly impractical.

And, yet, in July 2021 *Virgin Galactic* and *Blue Origin*, two privately owned spacecrafts, flew to near orbit altitudes and soft landed onto land. How did they do it? They came down slower. One problem solved.

Look carefully for people's underlying assumptions. What if an assumption could be changed? Approach this question imaginatively. For the moment don't get hung up on practicalities. What would be a potential result? Would it be good? If so, challenge yourself to find a way to change the underlying assumption.

Even very simple improvements, by changing an assumption, can lead to significant business innovations.

Levi Strauss received a patent for using a metal rivet to secure pockets to make pants more durable in 1873; this was the beginning of the blue jean.

The *Rothschild* banking business was started by Mayer Amschel Rothschild in the 18th Century. Mayer Rothschild's breakthrough innovation that transformed his business into an international banking powerhouse came about by setting up each of his five sons in Rothschild branches in major cities throughout Europe.

Snapple[22] had the idea of pre-packaging iced tea with added natural flavors. Customers loved the taste and convenience, and their business boomed. Today, many "me-too" competitors have jumped into this space, but *Snapple* still is a popular brand.

At the creative stage, don't limit your imagination. Let your imagination run. Don't be limited. A brilliant idea may occur.

Go Forth!

Now the Lord said to Abram, "Go from your country and your kindred and your father's house to the land that I will show you.

- Genesis 12:1

[22] *Snapple* was started by Leonard Marsh, Hyman Golden, and Arnold Greenberg in 1972. They sold the business 1991 for $100 million.

The Hebrew for "go forth" in the beginning of this chapter in *Genesis* is transliterated "*lech lecha*" and it implies "go to yourself"[23]. In other words, Abraham experienced a revelation.

When an entrepreneur experiences their "ah hah" moment for an innovative business idea it also is a revelation. It is inspirational. For the entrepreneur it is a "leap of faith" to "go forth" to start their business. They take a risk.

Notice, too, that *God* commanded Abraham to go forth. For Abraham it was imperative.

For the entrepreneur it is imperative to act. This doesn't mean that the business idea is a definite "go". It means that the idea should be seriously evaluated. Don't dismiss these innovative ideas!

New business successes stem from inspiration coupled with careful planning and excellent execution. Bringing a new business idea to fruition successfully takes courage and hard work.

Abraham's story embodies this kind of courage and shows exceptional commitment.

Imagine Abram's courage to go home and tell his wife, "Sarai, you won't believe what happened to me today. *God* spoke to me, a *God* who is superior to all the other gods. *God* told us to leave home. I don't know where, exactly. ("*God* knows where!") But don't worry, *God* promised to make us into a great nation.[24]"

Midrash gives us more detail about Abraham's revelation that there must be one *God* above all other gods. Abraham's family and the people around him were idol worshipers. Abram clearly did not go into his father's business, which the *Midrash* tells us was making idols.[25]

Sarai probably said something like, "*Meshugah"*, which is *Yiddish* for "crazy"!

---

[23] Rabbi Jack Bemporad, personal communication

[24] Genesis 12:2 with apologies for my paraphrasing.

[25] Abraham's life is described in *Genesis Rabbah* Chapter 38 which is considered classical Jewish text that was written between 300-500 CE

But the story gets even more *meshugah*. Abram further says to Sarai, "Oh by the way, you know the *God*, above all other gods, that I've been telling you about. Well, we're now changing our names, too. *God* told me so."

> *No longer shall your name be Abram, but your name shall be Abraham; for I have made you the father of a multitude of nations.*
>
> \- *Genesis 17:5*

> *And God said to Abraham, "As for Sar'ai your wife, you shall not call her name Sar'ai, but Sarah shall be her name.*
>
> \- *Genesis 17: 15*

And that is still not all. Abram, now called Abraham, literally put his manhood on the line to commit to his new venture.

> *And God said to Abraham, "As for you, you shall keep my covenant, you and your descendants after you throughout their generations.*
> *This is my covenant, which you shall keep, between me and you and your descendants after you: Every male among you shall be circumcised.*
>
> \- *Genesis* 17: 9-10

Go ahead and laugh! Abraham's ideas were way out there. His ideas also were profound and life changing.

This was a key turning point in history. Abraham's story became the *Genesis* for Judaism, and in turn Christianity and Islam. Abraham's idea that there must be a "*God* above all other gods" is monotheism. Judaism, Christianity and Islam are called the Abrahamic religions, because they each stem from this same ancestor and his brilliant idea.

Not only is there One *God*. *God* wants us to fulfill a higher purpose.

Do Good!

Humankind's "work" was redefined as fulfilling a higher purpose.[26]

This was very different from Adam's and Eve's labor. Adam's and Eve's work was simply to feed and clothe themselves and have children, in other words, "multiply".

The word "entrepreneur" didn't exist in Abraham's time[27], but Abraham acted like an entrepreneur. He came up with a new idea, and he implemented his idea. He had to shut out the critics and trust himself. He took a leap of faith.

Abraham had *chutzpah! (Chutzpah* is *Yiddish* with similar meaning as "hubris" or "audacity" in English. *Chutzpah,* though, sounds more onomatopoetic and funnier.)

Like Abraham, you should feel that your work is doing good which will give you long-lasting motivation. Your customers will see both the good that you do and your enthusiasm, and you will be rewarded.

> Don't take and get, like Adam and Eve.
>
> Give and receive, like Abraham and Sarah.

This is the essence of Jewish motivation.

Repair Your Business

> *Every person should see himself and the entire world as in a delicate balance, whereby any one deed can tip himself and the entire world towards the good.*
>
> -Maimonides[28]

Maimonides' statement teaches us *Tikkun Olam*, Hebrew meaning

---

[26] Judaism's first contribution was the belief in one *God*, or monotheism. Judaism also emphasized the idea that *God* was not just the origin of all existence, but *God* was the inspiration that Goodness should be shared by all humankind.
[27] "Entrepreneur" was utilized in Europe in the 18th century but took on the connotation of a business *go-getter* in the early 20th century. (Merriam – Webster)
[28] Maimonides, who lived in the 12th century, was one of Judaism's greatest scholars.

"repair the world". Humankind's challenge is to make the world a better place, to repair it. We repair the world by doing good deeds. Little good deeds add up.

Tikkun Olam is not just charity, although charity is certainly included. Making things better is a good approach in general. Little improvements add up to big benefits.

Modern business lingo calls this "continuous improvement". This is a meticulous practice of measuring processes for any defects; analyzing the causes of those defects; and prioritizing and proceeding to make corrective improvements.

You succeed in business by selling "goods", pun intended. You also succeed in business by selling services which people consider to be good.

Jews are known for being good doctors, dentists, lawyers, accountants, teachers, scientists, investment counselors, and members of other professions. Each of these professions require continuing education and continual improvement.

Similarly, good businessowners should never be fully satisfied with their products. They work to make their goods and their services better and better.

Continuous improvement takes passion, attention to details, and stick-to-it-ness. Done well, continuous improvement becomes a hallmark of a business that, in itself, can be a valuable differentiation.

Continuous improvement requires frank acknowledgement of those things in your business that are not as good as they could be. The business owner often must swallow their pride, admit their mistakes, or admit what they don't know.

> I had a boss who regularly held staff meetings attended by both his senior managers and a level or two of other managers. His motivation for these large meetings was to share knowledge and foster cooperation among departments. He often would go around the table and ask, "What is not going well in your department?" Most managers were reticent to answer, feeling that they should be in control of their departments. The boss would say, "Every department has things which can be improved. To be a good manager you must know what isn't going well."

Motivating your people to appreciate and focus on continuous improvement takes effort and leadership. Most people tend to be defensive and hide problems. Getting your team to bring mistakes and bad occurrences to the forefront so that they become learning experiences requires mutual trust. That is key to improving.

Superheroes?

> *There is only one who is all powerful, and his greatest weapon is love.*
>
> - Stan Lee, creator of Marvel comic books[29]

Business has winners and losers. The overall U.S. economy grows at a low single digit percentage, about 2 to 3% in a good year. Yet, individual businesses tend to set their growth goals much higher, say 6% to 10% or even higher. Obviously, something has to give. A lot of businesses don't meet their goals.

What distinguishes business winners?

A few businesses, call them either brilliant or lucky, have a product or service that is unique or in short supply and is highly desired. At least for the short term these businesses beat their competition. They seem like superheroes. They can do something that other businesses cannot do.

But there are no real superheroes. Business, in a free-enterprise economy, is not like a comic book. Every business has competition.

Even a business with a unique patent will face competition, eventually and sooner than they might think. Competitors will jump into their market niche with similar products.

> In the early automobile days, *Chevrolet* jumped in to mimic *Ford's* success.
>
> *Apple's* PC launched in 1976 was preceded by *Atari*, *Motorola* and *Radio Shack* portable computers.
>
> *IBM*'s PC came after *Apple*'s. *Samsung* followed *Apple* into smart phones.

---

[29] Stan Lee was born in 1922, nee Stanley Martin Lieber, of Romanian-born Jewish immigrant parents.

> "Me-too drugs"[30] are common in the pharmacological industry that break into the patent protection of a "first-in-class" drug.

Moreover, first-mover products in any industry also have the problem of teaching the buying public about the advantages of their new product. And, they usually have problems of scaling up to balance their product delivery capabilities with their infrastructure.

Good and successful products attract new competitors. Ultimately, every business has competition.

Of course, you want your business to develop products and services that are unique and better. And, where feasible it's beneficial to get a patent or trademark to guard your uniqueness.

With or without patent-type protection, there are two ways to beat your competition. You can either beat your competition on the *basics* or beat them on *details.*

> *Basic* competition: "We promise to do such-and-such for you, and nobody else can do what we do."

> *Details* competition: "We do it better than others. We make you, our customer, feel more welcome, safer, confident, happier as part of the experience".

Both strategies to compete, "basic" and "details" are powerful.

Basic competition is compelling if it is true, or true enough. *Levi Strauss* jeans don't come apart. *Google* is a great search engine. *Zabars Delicatessen* has New York's best whitefish salad.

Lower cost also could be part of your basic competitive strategy, but competing only based on low cost is risky. It could set-off a race to the bottom with competitors slashing prices in a back-and-forth battle. Notice the difference in these ad taglines.

> "Levi Strauss jeans will cost you less, because you won't have to replace them."

> "Buy your men's suit from Marty's[31], and get one free."

---

[30] A pharmacologically active compound that is structurally related to a first-in-class compound. (British Journal of Clinical Pharmacology March 2020)

[31] A fictional store

The Levi Strauss advantage is sustainable. It's a real product advantage. The Marty's ad almost demands that the neighboring men's store also announce a similar sale, with the result that the margins for both stores will suffer.

After college I worked for Insurance Company of North America (INA) which prided themselves on being creative. Someone suggested that we put our products on sale, temporarily lower prices to increase market share.

Paul L., INA's Chief Actuary, put the argument to bed saying, "That would be like "Green Stamps". If we do that our competitors will have to match our move. We'll be stuck with lower prices in the industry with no advantage for any company."

Green Stamps was a retail gimmick in the Fifties. Retailers gave out *Green Stamps* which could be accumulated and redeemed for household goods. As a kid my mother gave me the job of putting *Green Stamps* into the booklets that were provided by the S&H Company that handled the redemption process. *Green Stamps* went away, but food markets still utilize lots of coupons which can be redeemed at checkout.

Did *Green Stamps* make sense? Do food markets' coupons make sense? Coupons lower prices, raises the stores' processing costs, and since competitors offer similar coupons there is no real advantage for any store. Coupons also are a bit of a hassle for consumers.

Innovation needed?

Price Club was founded in 1976 by Sol Price. *Costco* was formed in 1983 by Jeffrey Brotman and Jim Sinegal[32]. These two companies merged in 1993. Today, *Costco* is publicly owned and is one of the largest retailers. *Costco*'s innovation is to charge a membership fee and offer discounted goods that are essentially always on sale.

You can develop product or service innovations that really differentiate your offering. You may discover ways to truly reduce your costs which would allow you a real pricing advantage.

Work hard but work smart. When you have a product advantage take

---

[32] Sol Price and Jeff Brotman were raised in Jewish families. Jim Sinegal was raised Catholic.

advantage of it. But keep in mind that product advantages tend to get copied, or even leap-frogged, by competitors.

Stan Lee's quote at the beginning of this section implies that *God* is the "only one who is all powerful". Perhaps, but for us mortals nothing is all powerful. Everything can be improved, so never stop improving your products.

Stan Lee also mentions "love". Be kind. Be gentle. Those are ways to show love to your customers that every business can aspire to do.

Put It To Work

Asah (Do)

- Get your creative juices flowing regularly. Exercise, meditate, or pray - or all three.
- Look for problems. They always exist. Prioritize the problems and fix them one at a time.
- Reward your employees for spotting problems. That is the first step to continuously improve.
- Strive to make your product so unique that you have a monopoly, at least for a time. But don't count on it.
- If your business is fortunate to become a "super-hero", even for a while, thank God for your success. Pay it back and forward.

Bara (Create)

- You will face turning points at various time throughout your career, such as changing age or health or business conditions. Recognize these turning points. Try to make them opportunities.
- Look for what is good and purposeful in your work. That is how you find and sustain motivation.
- Know that every decision entails risk. But, at the end of the day, "Go forth". That will always take a "leap of faith". Trust yourself.

- Realize that it's not easy nor comfortable to take a position - that is different from the norm. Get comfortable with your inspiration.

- Leverage your creative strengths.

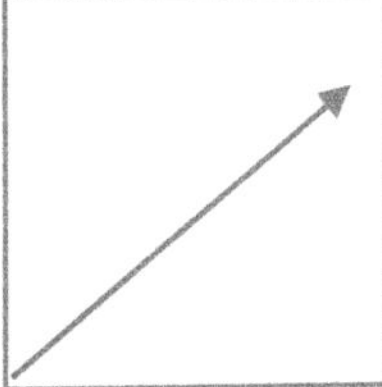

Till the Garden: Tool Kit

> *You shall remember the Lord your God, for it is he who gives you power to get wealth; that he may confirm his covenant which he swore to your fathers, as at this day.*
>
> \- *Deuteronomy* 8:18

Before we go to work, we need the proper tools, and we need to know how to utilize them.

"Business" and "money" are tools. These are human inventions, which we utilize to do commerce more efficiently.

"Science" and "technology" are also key tools. Science provides a methodology to observe and learn about natural phenomena. "Technology" is an invention that helps us adapt to our environment.

Judaism considers all these tools to be gifts from *God*. Humans uniquely have been given the gift of intelligence with which we developed these tools.

Human life is unimaginable without these tools. We've made these tools better throughout the centuries, but humans utilized these tools since ancient times.

Tools can do good. They can create value. But tools also can be misused, which can be dangerous and destroy value.

Jewish wisdom teaches about our human obligation to utilize tools to do good. And Jewish wisdom also has a lot to say about how we, humans, should be mindful of the limitations of any of these tools.

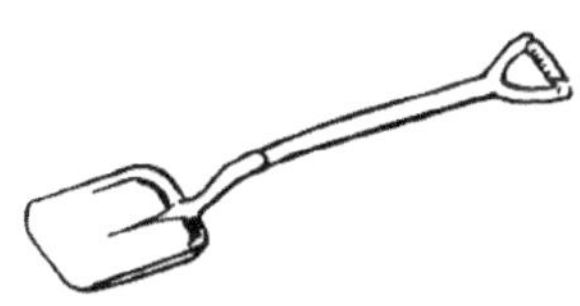

Money Makes the World Go Round[33]

> *You shall love the Lord your God with all your heart, and with all your soul, and with all your might.*
>
> - *Deuteronomy* 6:5

Your love for *God* should exceed all material things.

Sure, money is important. Jews do not begrudge anyone having a lot of money, and in fact, Jewish knowledge properly practiced will greatly increase your chances to enjoy material wealth.

But chasing money is misguided.

> *He who loves money will not be satisfied with money; nor he who loves wealth, with gain: this also is vanity.*
>
> - *Ecclesiastes* 5:10

Appreciate that money, itself, is a human invention, a kind of technology. Money technology has changed, and ostensibly improved, throughout history. And money technology will continue to change.

Before money was invented people bartered to "buy" things. Suppose I am a farmer who has fig trees, and you are a hunter who just caught a large animal fit to eat. Let's trade. How many figs do I have to give you to get meat that will feed my family for a week?

Bartering was very inefficient and complicated. The hunter needs to hire a butcher to clean and cut the animal into portions. The farmer with fig trees wants meat now, but his crop won't be harvested for another few months. And, if the hunter and the farmer live in villages only a few miles apart, getting together to inspect and trade their respective goods gets difficult.

Money was a necessary invention to make trading easier. In retrospect, money seems obvious, but at the time it was a brilliant insight that

---

[33] Lyrics to song from "Cabaret", 1966 musical by John Kander and Fred Ebb, two Jewish stars on the Broadway scene.

improved human life.

The earliest money probably was an informal agreement between people to trade something of value that the society in that area considered valuable. For example, shells were used as money as early as 1200 BCE.

Coins may not have appeared in the Middle East until about 550 BCE. Coins were an innovation that required the government to define and produce the "coins of the realm". To buy something you had to utilize a coin sanctioned by the government and recognize that a particular coin had a specified amount of value.

Bills obviously are easier to carry around. This was another invention. The government had to print the bill, make it so that it was difficult to counterfeit, and convince the populace that the bill stood for a certain amount of coin. Initially, bills represented a certain amount of gold.

In 1933 the U.S. eliminated the gold standard for domestic transactions. Essentially, the U.S. government said, "This paper money is still worth a dollar. Just keep using it as you did before, even though you cannot turn it into the government for gold". In 1971 the U.S. government eliminated the gold standard for international transactions. The value of a dollar is based upon the trust that we place in it as a trading instrument.

International banking is necessary for worldwide business. Banks regularly transfer money and trade currencies which links the world's economies. Banks require strict adherence to established guidelines and rules to move money among accounts and across country borders.

International banking is relatively modern. The Rothschild bank which began in the 1760's was among the first to establish branches in major capitals across Europe. Besides facilitating cross border trade, the Rothschilds became trusted advisors to business leaders throughout Europe.

Our concepts of money continue to change. New inventions, such as *ApplePay* and *Venmo* and *Zelle*, are replacing how we think of money. We are much less dependent upon our current location when it comes to doing business. We can invest and transact business digitally from almost anywhere and essentially instantly. Currencies still are nation based, but since each currency can be readily converted to U.S. dollars the dollar still is the *de facto* worldwide currency standard. However, there are rumblings about an international currency, and cryptocurrency may be emerging to fill that type of need.

Jewish wisdom distinguishes between money, itself, and what we do with our money.

Money is a tool. It is a means to facilitate business. The value in money is that we can substitute it for goods and services or deploy it to build a business that produces goods or services.

Since money, by itself, is just a symbol, worshipping money is akin to idol worship. It is misguided.

Rather, we are taught to pray for the insight and strength to utilize our money to do good. Do good with your money. Trust that more money will follow so that you can do more good.

Science: Observe and Learn

> *Happy is the man who finds wisdom, and the man who gets understanding, for the gain from it is better than gain from silver and its profit better than gold. She is more precious than jewels, and nothing you desire can compare with her.*
>
> \- *Proverbs* 3:13-15

We've discussed previously that *God* spoke to Abraham. For Abraham it was a great insight that changed his life.

At the time people worshipped many gods. As a boy we may presume that Abraham accepted what his parents and teachers taught him. There was a god of the rivers, a god of the sky, and so on. That explained the world[34].

But Abraham challenged the conventional thinking of that time. Even if each part of nature was ruled by a different god, Abraham reasoned, "What ruled the gods?'

Abraham was a "scientist", even before "science" was part of our language. Like a scientist, Abraham keenly observed nature. He tried to explain what he saw based upon existing theory.

What does a scientist do when existing theory doesn't work? Answer: Modify the theory.

When an experiment or discovery contradicts existing theories, it is thrilling. For scientists, it signifies that they are potentially on the verge of learning something new. That is how a new hypothesis is formed.

When an experimental outcome contradicts existing theory the first thing a scientist does is repeat the experiment. They want to be sure that their observation of nature is accurate. Scientists also publish their findings, including a detailed description of their experiments, so other scientists can repeat the same experiments to verify the findings.

What Abraham did was genius, and it took courage. Imagine telling your parents, friends and neighbors that their ideas, their religious beliefs, are wrong. We can surmise that his audiences initially were skeptical, perhaps dismissive, and perhaps even made angry. How dare Abraham tell them that the idols to which they were praying were false gods.

Abraham was not trying to start a religion. He was being observant - of nature.

Scientists and religionists have clashed throughout history including within the Jewish and Christian communities. Galileo and Spinoza, both of whom lived in the 17th century, are famous examples of this.

> Galileo performed brilliant observations of the heavens that confirmed Copernicus' theory that the earth revolves around the sun, not the other way around. Galileo was punished by the Catholic

[34] *Genesis Rabbah – Midrashic* text written between 300-500 CE.

> Church in 1632 for espousing ideas that the church perceived as conflicting with their view of biblical creationism.
>
> Spinoza, a Jewish philosopher living in Amsterdam, was one of the most original and influential thinkers of his time. He did not deny the existence of *God*, but he challenged the view that the Bible was divinely written. He equated *God* with *Nature*. Spinoza's synagogue expelled him for this supposed heresy.

When Einstein, the most famous scientist in the 20th century, was asked about his religious views he famously said, "I believe in Spinoza's *God* who reveals himself in the orderly harmony of what exists, not in a *God* who concerns himself with fates and actions of human beings".

Jewish knowledge in this book would be familiar to learned Jews from Orthodox and Reform congregations. Presumptuously, Spinoza and Einstein also would agree with the Jewish knowledge explained in this book. Indeed, many learned Christians would recognize many of the lessons in this book.

The scientific explanations in this book help to elucidate Jewish wisdom and demonstrate the relevance of Jewish wisdom to contemporary business. To me, there is no conflict between Judaism and science, although that personal point of view may be more familiar among more progressive Jewish audiences. Inclusion of these scientific analogies hopefully is not perceived by any religiously observant Jew as disrespectful.

Be observant of nature. Learn from nature.

Focus on the similarities between *Torah* and science. Focusing on the differences, I think, is counterproductive. For me, focusing on the similarities leads to insight and spiritual fulfillment.

Science Begets Technology

> *When the woman saw that the tree was good for food, and that it was a delight to the eyes, and that the tree was to be desired to*

make one wise, she took of its fruit and ate; and she also gave some to her husband, and he ate. Then the eyes of both were opened, and they knew that they were naked; and they sewed fig leaves together and made themselves aprons.

- *Genesis* 3:6-7

Adam and Eve demonstrated Free Will by eating the fruit from the forbidden tree. God had told them not to do so, but they did it anyway. Eating the fruit[35] gave Adam and Eve knowledge, so that humans, now, had a higher level of existence than any other animal.

But knowledge has consequences. The idyllic existence in Eden ended. Humans don't just forage for food. Humans consciously act upon the environment to improve human living conditions.

Put differently, knowledge leads to science which leads to technology. Science is the study of nature and how natural things behave. Technology applies scientific findings to develop inventions that make things better.

When Adam and Eve were banished from the garden of Eden, they had to provide for themselves.

And the Lord God made for Adam and for his wife garments of skins and clothed them.

- *Genesis* 3.21

Clothing was the first technology, and it literally was a gift from *God*. Adam and Eve learned by this example that technology was a way to modify their environment to improve their existence.

Adam and Eve got dressed, to go out in public so to speak, and something else profound happened. They discovered modesty. Whether modesty is good or bad is arguable, but from the very beginning we see that technology has consequences - potentially both good and bad. Some consequences of technology are predictable, but some consequences are unforeseen.

Throughout human history technology has altered how we live, and no

[35] Later literature and artwork depict the fruit as an apple. The Hebrew text suggests that the fruit may have been a fig. Either way, the context and meaning are the same.

surprise, our industries and businesses have changed significantly with each major technological breakthrough.

Prehistoric man witnessed fire in the natural world, perhaps when they saw lightning strike dried vegetation. In time, humans developed the technology to control fire, to transport fire, and eventually to ignite fire when and where they desired. Their "industry" changed dramatically. Food, housing, and clothing, the most personal basic products, changed profoundly.

Who invented the wheel? The oldest wheel found in archeological executions was found in Mesopotamia and believed to be over 5,500 years old. That wheel was used for a potter's wheel, not transportation.[36] It took another creative invention, the axle, to adapt the wheel for transportation.

Farming was another huge leap forward in technology. Humans began to domesticate animals for transportation and agriculture. With this technology, humans could stay put on their land, not just roam to hunt for food.

The printing press came much later[37]. Knowledge could now be cheaply and widely disseminated. Perhaps more than anything printing technology led to the end of the Dark Ages and ushered in the Renaissance. Economics and the very nature of business changed.

Today, we live in the "computer age" or perhaps more accurately the "digital age" since this technology is now in our autos, appliances, machinery, medical devices, and so on. But history shows that computerization is not the first technological wave which has had a huge impact on business, and it won't be the last. 100 years, or so, ago we would have been focusing on electricity and its influences on modern business. In a decade from now we may focus more on biotechnology, and perhaps further in the future on space travel.

Computerization, though, is still hugely important for business planning. Industries still are being created that utilize computers in new ways, and businesses are falling by the wayside due to obsolescence or simply because they are not utilizing computers effectively.

Artificial Intelligence (AI) is a current iteration of how computer

---

[36] Mary Bellis December 20, 2020, published on thoughtco.com

[37] The Gutenberg printing press appeared in 1439.

technology is impacting our lives.

Technology impacts the bottom line for all businesses, and always has. Technology is everyone's responsibility. Like everything, think of technology as a gift and a tool to do Good.

Long Lasting Companies

> *Someone's sitting in the shade today because someone planted a tree a long time ago.*
>
> *- Warren Buffett*[38]

The longer a scientific theory holds sway the greater is the tendency to accept the "truth" behind that scientific theory. Remember to a scientist, "truth" is what is consistent with experimental observation. As observations build up over time and technology is developed based upon a particular theory the theory gains more and more acceptance.

Something similar happens in business. The longer a company is successful in business that company builds up barriers against new competitors. The long-standing successful company builds up resources, including money, institutional knowledge, and reputation.

In the 1960's and 1970's the "nifty-fifty" was an informal name given to a group of roughly 50 stocks that were regarded as solid "buy-and-hold" stocks. Most of those companies are still operating, and Howard Marks and Jeremy Siegel, both famous Jewish financial analysts and authors, have shown that these companies have returned reasonable, although not necessarily out-sized, financial returns. Examples of the "nifty-fifty" include: Proctor & Gamble, Coca-Cola, American Express, IBM, and Johnson & Johnson.

Jews are rightfully proud that Judaism has stood the test of time. Throughout history Jews have been discriminated and persecuted, and yet Jews and Judaism has survived.

See the wisdom in tradition. Traditions exist and have flourished, because they represent some underlying truths.

---

[38] Warren Buffett is not Jewish. His emphasis on building long-term value rather than idolizing money, however, is characteristic of Jewish wisdom.

"If you walk in my statutes and observe my commandments and do them, then I will give you your rains in their season, and the land shall yield its increase, and the trees of the field shall yield their fruit.

- *Leviticus* 26:3-4

Put It To Work

Asah (Do)

- Pay attention to business growth. When your business is not growing figure out what isn't going well. Is your business not attracting enough new customers? Are existing customers not re-buying? is there an innovation that is better than your product?
- How could you make your business process, or a portion of it, faster or cheaper or with more quality?
- Encourage constructive criticism. Be open-minded to spot problems or to become aware of potential innovations.

Bara (Create)

- Concentrate on whether the business, and your role within it, are doing good for humankind. Do good, and money follows.
- Keenly observe what is going on within your business.
- Recognize that new things always come along, and business is continually changing. Evaluate whether and how new ways of doing business can improve upon how things were done before.
- Assist the business structure and processes to adapt to these better ways. Allow yourself some patience while things are improving. Get energized by how the future can be better.

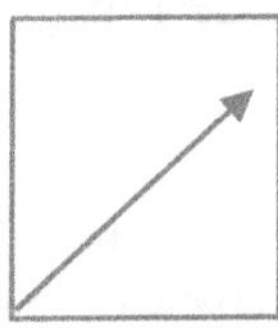

Employ God's Gift of Knowledge

And they said to one another, "Come, let us make bricks, and burn them thoroughly." And they had brick for stone, and bitumen for mortar.

- *Genesis* 11:3

This is from the story of the *Tower of Babel*. It is a story about technology advancement and the misuse of that technology.

Prior to this time, humans made their habitats out of stone. Brick was new, an invention. It was stone-like, and it had advantages over stone in that it could be layered more readily to build high walls - and a tower.

According to *Midrash*, which are rabbinic stories that expand upon the text in *Torah*, when a person fell off the tower and died nobody cared. However, if a brick fell and cracked, they all stopped to mourn the lost brick[39].

Another *Midrash*[40] is that Abraham watched the building of the tower, and he saw the lack of deeper meaning. He understood that a building with no higher purpose is dangerous. He realized that humanity's purpose cannot merely be to make a name for itself, to achieve material success.

Remember the *Babel* story. Misusing technology to get rich with no other good purpose doesn't work in the long run.

Technology is a gift from *God*. We must remember that. When we invent and utilize technology, we are obligated to use it for good.

---

[39] chabad.org "The Tower of Technology"

[40] chabad.org "The Tower of Babel: What Was Up With It?"

Technology - Good and Bad

You shall keep my statutes. You shall not let your cattle breed with a different kind; you shall not sow your field with two kinds of seed; nor shall there come upon you a garment of cloth made of two kinds of stuff.

- *Leviticus* 19:19

Generally, we think of technology as a good thing. But, just as nothing that is human made is perfect, technology can have negative consequences. Technology can be bad when:1) It is used in the wrong way, or 2) When it is over utilized.

Kilayim is a Hebrew expression meaning "two kinds together". Judaism's sacred texts describe prohibitions against combining certain plants and animals together and go into detail about what is *kilayim* and what isn't.

Today, these discussions may seem arcane for most Jews. Ancient Jewish writings applied spiritual principles to agriculture, since agriculture was the modern technology in those times. However, the essence of that Jewish knowledge applies today, including how to consider utilizing our modern computer, biotech, and other technologies.

Kilayim prohibitions provide guidelines that respect God's creation *versus* what humans invent or develop.

Then God said, "Let us make man in our image, after our likeness; and let them have dominion over the fish of the sea, and over the birds of the air, and over the cattle, and over all the earth, and over every creeping thing that creeps upon the earth."

- *Genesis* 1:26

God created the different species, and so only *God* can create new species.

Humans have dominion over other creatures. Humans can herd and breed animals; cultivate trees and plants; and so on. But all our dominion still belongs to *God*.

Human inventions seek to be *God*-like, but we must be humble. We cannot see *God*, and we cannot fully understand *God. God* encourages us to be creative, but we continually look to *God* to seek understanding. We pray to *God* continually for inspiration as well as to remind ourselves that we don't know what we cannot know. We cannot fully foresee the future.

As technology has become more complicated, so too are there growing complexities about what use of technology goes too far. Consider, for example, these currently hotly debated topics:

> Artificial Intelligence (AI) - Are students permitted to utilize AI for their own essays? How should media control AI developed images that mimic someone else, potentially for malicious purposes?
>
> Bio-engineered agricultural products - Are Non-GMO (genetically modified organisms) foods safer? Are genetically modified seeds a good thing? Should we genetically modify insects and release them into the wild to control insect pests?
>
> Vaccines - Are vaccines that are bio-engineered safe? Should government, businesses, or educational institutions insist on participants in their establishments being vaccinated to control disease outbreaks?
>
> Human Embryo intervention - When is it okay to treat a human *in utero*? When is it okay for a woman to terminate a pregnancy?

The tradeoffs in these debates are not easy. Informed Jews may have differing points of view about any of these issues.

Jews have always intrinsically understood both the value of technology and its limitations. Our context always comes back to the idea that *God* is the Creator, and humankind's abilities to create is a privileged gift from *God*. Always we must endeavor to ensure that our creativity serves to improve the world that *God* gave us.

Jewish teaching methods exemplify debating both sides of an issue, looking at positive and negative potential consequences. Jews excel at this type of debate, in part based upon training in this approach in *Talmud* study.

The thorny questions about technology and how to deploy technology should be approached in the same way. Often there will be no obvious best answer. Explore pros and cons from various angles.

Be like an informed Jew and ask, "What does *God* intend that we do?"

Technology - Too Much of a Good Thing Is Bad

> *All the able men who were doing every sort of task on the sanctuary came, each from the task that he was doing, and said to Moses, "The people bring much more than enough for doing the work which the Lord has commanded us to do."*
> *So Moses gave command, and word was proclaimed throughout the camp, "Let neither man nor woman do anything more for the offering for the sanctuary." So the people were restrained from bringing;*
>
> \- *Exodus 36:4-6*

After Moses brought the Ten Commandments down from Mount Sinai, the people set about building the Sanctuary. You would think nothing would be too good for this endeavor. And, indeed, the people enthusiastically and generously brought gifts to be used to build the sanctuary. When their donations became too extravagant Moses necessarily set limitations.

Wine is good example of how a good thing taken to excess becomes bad. Jews traditionally toast events with wine and recite a blessing to sanctify and rejoice at these events. Wine symbolizes prosperity and joy. Each *Shabbat*, sabbath, Jews usher in the Sabbath with a prayer over wine. Similarly, at each Jewish wedding the bride and groom ceremoniously sip from one glass of wine.

Purim is a Jewish holiday that celebrates the Hebrews becoming free from Persian persecution about 2500 years ago. The Hebrews at that time were rightfully ecstatic in their celebration. Today, as part of the *Purim* celebration, Jews allow themselves to get drunk on wine, symbolizing how happy we are to be free of persecution. This is the only time during the year when a Jew is permitted to become inebriated. Still, even at *Purim*, there are guidelines. Even on *Purim* Jews should not be drunk if they have responsibilities that day that would prevent them from being in adequate control of themselves, such as a physician or transportation worker or machine operator needs to be.[41]

So it is with technology, even excellent technologies. Like anything, a good thing taken to extremes or utilized too much crosses over to being bad.

Consider these examples from recent human history, just a few of many, illustrating how a good thing can become a bad thing when over-done.

> In the American West, the plains Indians hunted buffalo, and they utilized many parts of the buffalo in their economy, including for warm clothing. Indian tribes co-existed with buffalo for many years, and the buffalo was honored in their traditions. However, non-Indian hunters almost wiped out the buffalo herds, almost to extinction, after the American Civil War by over-hunting. These hunters didn't just hunt the buffalo for profit; their behavior got way out of hand as they slaughtered the buffalo as a blood-thirsty, malicious sport.
>
> Coatings, like plastic, were in use in the 1800's or earlier. The earliest sources of this type of material were from natural sources such as horn, tortoiseshell, and rubber. Bakelite, a very hard plastic, was utilized in the early 1900's for telephones. During WWII many additional plastics were developed, and in the 1950's and 1960's synthetic plastic products became ubiquitous in commercial and consumer products. Today, we realize that plastics don't breakdown readily in nature, and the disposal of plastics has become a significant problem in landfills and in the oceans.
>
> Social media is a relatively new technology.[42] Today, we stay in touch with one another via our cell phones; we text each other using shorthand acronyms; and we research investments, movies, books and other products by reading recommendations on the Internet. We now also realize that many people over-utilize these types of media. We especially worry that teenagers are overly influenced by popular show business and sports figures. We worry about sexual misconduct, financial scams, and other misuses of social media.

How do we know when a technology's usefulness is at its limits? When does too much of a good thing become bad?

---

[41] Chabad.org, "Do I Have to Get Drunk on Purim"

[42] 72% of American adults used some form of social media in 2019, up from 5% in 2005, the year after Facebook went live. (Pew Research Center)

There are no easy answers here. Some technologies are so new and changing so fast that it is very difficult to foresee how that technology will impact our society or our environment.

Jewish wisdom, informed by Jewish tradition, however, helps us to consider these questions.

> *You shall kindle no fire in all your habitations on the sabbath day."*
>
> - *Exodus 35:3*

Shabbat, Hebrew for sabbath, is not just a day of rest from work. *Shabbat* is a time for reflection. Our worship of *God* is filled with awe and thankfulness. We rest on Shabbat because *God* rested on the seventh day. We also challenge ourselves to be more *God*-like by doing our part to make the world better.

Religious Jews refrain from using electricity, a form of technology, on *Shabbat*. Orthodox rabbis have interpreted starting an electrical appliance as akin to kindling a fire, which is considered "work". You may not practice this tradition, but when you understand its origin and how it relates to the proper use of technology, you should admire the beauty and harmony of this tradition.

Pardon the following personification of *God*, but imagine *God* saying, "I gave you the gift of technology, and it's good that you are using technology properly in your work. But today stop working! Put aside your technology. Think about the source of your technology. Think about how when you go back to work you will help to make the world a better place. That is why I gave you the gift of technology in the first place."

We understand that all technologies have limitations.

> Are we being alert to how technology impacts people and our environment?
>
> Have we put into place safeguards so that technology is not over-utilized.?
>
> Have we trained people adequately to use technology properly?
>
> Have we protected people, including our children, from potential

mishaps involving technology?

Technology - Not Just for Geeks

And behold, I have taken your brethren the Levites from among the people of Israel; they are a gift to you, given to the Lord, to do the service of the tent of meeting.

- *Numbers* 18:6

God chose Aaron and his sons to be accountable to take care of the Tent of Meeting, the place where the Ten Commandment tablets were held in the Holy Tabernacle. The duties of the Levis, as Aaron's descendants were called, were very specific, and no other tribes were permitted to do this work. This was the technical work at the time. The Levis were the first technical geek-squad.

Today, we endearingly refer to technical computer people as "geeks". These technicians are trained to fix computer hardware and software problems, whereas most of us are content, even afraid, to open a computer, change component parts, or alter software configurations. We, the non-geeks that is, don't want to break things or make apparent problems worse.

Technological change, indeed, is occurring rapidly, and there is growing demand for people trained in computer science[43]. Professionals trained in computer science are in demand in all companies, across all types of businesses. CIO (Chief Information Officer) has become an executive level position, the person who manages the computer department but also participates in corporate strategy as computerization is transforming

[43] Computer and Information Science is the fourth most-popular master's degree. (Fortune, December 2022)

almost every industry.

But guess what? You also must become at least somewhat proficient with computers. Computers are important for your job, in your function, no matter what you do. Computerization is not just for the geek squad.

Also, computer geeks, and again I mean that term endearingly, are usually so heads-down working on their technology that they may not see the big picture clearly. There are many leadership and managerial roles, other than, say, programming, necessary to develop and build wealth with a particular technology.

It also takes wisdom, long-term thinking, and sensitivity to assess when technology is being over utilized or used for bad purposes.

> Robert Oppenheimer led the development of the atomic bomb at Los Alamos. Oppenheimer was a brilliant physicist and a very capable leader. The atomic bomb may not have been built at all without his leadership[44].
>
> Oppenheimer was raised in a Jewish family, but his parents did not celebrate Judaism traditionally. Oppenheimer attended the Ethical Culture Society on New York's Upper West Side which was an offshoot of Reform Judaism. Oppenheimer learned universal moral principles consistent with Jewish teachings, though he was not schooled particularly in Jewish practices. He felt strongly that science and technology must serve the well-being of the whole of society.
>
> Oppenheimer thought deeply about the moral justification for building the bomb. He knew that Germany was working on the same technology, and he thought it was imperative that America invent that technology first.
>
> After WWII Oppenheimer argued vehemently that the U.S. should set up an international organization to control and manage atomic energy. He believed that would be the only way to prevent an arms race between the U.S. and Russia. His stance against the military establishment led to him being ousted from his position on the Atomic Energy Commission.

---

[44] Kai Bird and Martin Sherwin, American Prometheus: The Triumph and Tragedy of J. Robert Oppenheimer, Atlantic Books, January 2009

Oppenheimer's inner conflict about the development of atomic energy makes his story so interesting. Whether Oppenheimer made the right judgements during WWII and afterwards can be argued both ways.

Computerization is not the only technology. Accounting is a type of business technology, and everyone in business should understand some rudimentary accounting. You should know, for example, how to read an income statement or to evaluate a balance sheet.

Each industry has its own technology, and you should understand the basics of technology utilized by your company. For example, if you work in pharmacology learn some basic principles of biology and chemistry even if you are not a biologist, physician or chemist.

Try to see the big picture. How are computers changing your industry? What are the other key technologies impacting your industry?

In your role, even if it is not in a technical field *per se*, how does the technology impact your department? How do you anticipate that you will need to adapt to a new technology?

Technology is too important to be left to the engineers.

Put It To Work

Asah (Do)

- On Shabbat, or your Sabbath, stop to rejoice in all the goodness that you enjoy. Be in awe of the technology that makes your life better. Challenge yourself to add to that goodness in your own work.

- Anything done to excess is not good. Don't forget that technology, as important and useful as it is, can be overly utilized or utilized improperly.

- Don't leave technology to the technologists. It's too important for your business, and sometimes leads to enormous breakthroughs. Intentionally make technological innovation part of your business planning, no matter what business you are in.

Bara (Create)

- Remind yourself that any technology is ultimately a gift from God, and our responsibility is to utilize this gift is to improve the world.
- Even a very good thing, has downsides. Minimize and mitigate those costs.
- Don't leave technology to the technologists. Getting technology to be practical and marketable takes many skills.
- Help your employees to adapt to new technologies. Involve everyone in the efforts to improve on your technology marketing message and fulfillment.
- Complex modern technologies raise complicated tradeoffs. Be open-minded about positive and negative consequences of how we deploy technology.
- Don't be intimidated by technology. Ask questions. Take charge of how computerization, or any new technology, will impact your job; your department; your company.
- Keep learning. Whatever you learned in college will be obsolete by the time you retire. Invest the time to keep your skills current.

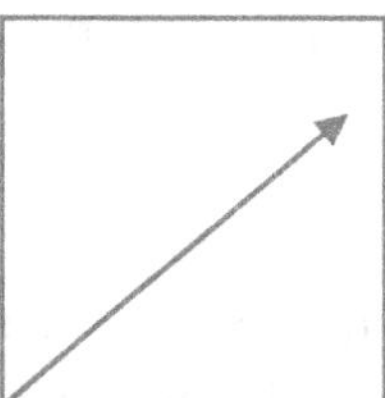

Judge With Wisdom

You cannot see my face; for man shall not see me and live.

- *Exodus* 33:20

This was *God*'s response to Moses when Moses asked on Mt. Sinai to see *God's* glory.

We cannot "see" *God.* We cannot fully understand *God. God* proclaimed his name to Moses, but we don't know *God*'s name. Jews refer to *God* as *Adonai*, which is translated as Lord. Orthodox Jews say Hashem, which simply means "The Name".

Isaiah, a Hebrew prophet who lived in the 8th century BCE, similarly taught:

> *For my thoughts are not your thoughts, neither are your ways my ways, says the Lord.*

- *Isaiah* 55:8

We can follow *God's mitzvoth*, commandments, but knowing *God* fully is beyond our human capacities.

Usually, we can judge right from wrong, good from bad, but we encounter human situations for which this judgement is not especially clear. Colloquially we say, "The situation is not black or white; it is shades of gray."

For these difficult situations we apply teachings from *Torah* as best we can.

Shades of Gray

What is "Right and Good"

> *And you shall do what is right and good in the sight of the Lord, that it may go well with you, and that you may go in and take possession of the good land which the Lord swore to give to your fathers*
>
> \- *Deuteronomy* 6:18

Maimonides, a rabbi and philosopher who became one of the most prolific and influential *Torah* scholars in the Middle Ages, wrote commentaries pertaining to each verse in *Torah*. For the verse quoted above, Maimonides wrote, in part, "This is a great principle, for it is impossible to mention in the *Torah* all aspects of man's conduct with his neighbors and friends, and all his various transactions, and the ordinances of all societies and countries."

Clearly, there many verses in *Torah* that explicitly state what to do or what not to do. But, as Maimonides wrote, there are instances that we encounter for which it may not be so clear what *Torah* teaches. So, what should we do?

We could, and should, consult with our Rabbis who are better schooled on *Torah* than we may be ourselves. Rabbis also are more familiar with *Torah* commentaries written by renowned former rabbis, such as Maimonides.

Abraham Isaac Kook, known as Rav Kook, was an Orthodox rabbi who was Chief Rabbi of British Palestine, just before the rebirth of the Nation of Israel in 1948. Rav Kook, wrote, "We must hold ourselves accountable to not merely follow authorities but to make hard moral decisions on our own after consulting other forms of wisdom. . . May we all take in so much wisdom from the *Torah*, from our souls, from others, and from the world to the point that we are overflowing, and then may we have the courage to do the hardest job of all: tap into our deepest intellectual and spiritual faculties and make difficult, moral choices."

Judaism asks that you think for yourself. You are obligated to study *Torah,* and you are encouraged to connect with *God* yourself. In the end, when faced with a difficult moral dilemma ask yourself, "What do you think *God* would want you to do?"

Unfortunately, it may be rare when a corporate officer or director

> says, "Let's do what is right and good." Nobody at work mentions *God*, as we have been trained to separate religion from secular situations.
>
> On many occasions I've heard someone in corporate leadership say, "How will the street (meaning Wall Street) react?" Or "Which decision will make more money?"

There is a huge opportunity for businesses to bridge the cultural divide between spiritual teachings that most of us experience and how we apply that spiritual background to our day-to-day business activities.

> Once at my synagogue we were confronted with an unprecedented moral situation. The rabbi was unavailable, and it was up to me and another synagogue leader to decide. I suggested, "Let's do what *God* would want us to do." The other leader said, "Great. That is such a refreshing and good approach." We both left that meeting feeling good about our decision.

Presume *God* is watching. Do what is right and good in the sight of the Lord. Use that approach, and you will be led to a good decision.

Priorities

Sometimes what is "good" is not so clear. In fact, a lot of the time there are tradeoffs to be considered. How do you weigh the tradeoffs?

> *If I am not for myself, who will be for me? If I am only for myself, what am I? And if not now, when?"*
>
> - Hillel, a great Jewish sage who died c.10 CE

It is not necessarily selfish to prioritize yourself first. Consider these examples:

> In an airline emergency we are instructed by flight attendants to put the oxygen mask on ourselves before tending to our traveling companion, including a small child. Not many of us face this sort of emergency, thank *God*, and it's hard to imagine how we would react in such a situation. Mothers, acting on instinct, for example may rush to save their small child.
>
> Years ago, I was trained to be a lifeguard. We were taught to

approach a drowning victim in such a way that the victim, in their panic, wouldn't grab and drown the both of us.

Physicians, nurses, and other medical personnel are trained and are diligent to wear masks, gowns, gloves and other protective equipment when treating a patient. This protects the patient from infection, but importantly it protects the medical provider from getting sick themselves.

"Be good to yourself is a top priority". We cannot be good to another if we, ourselves, are not at our best.

After you take care of yourself, what is next?

Seek good for yourself.

Seek good for an other.

Seek good for all others.

Seek good for future generations.

Seek good for all Life and Creation.

Seek good by continuously improving.

- Rabbi Michael Shevack[45]

After we take care of ourselves, it's natural to take care of our own family. And, after our biologic family, we should take care of our business family.

You owe loyalty to the business where you currently work. This brings up its own complications. Any business requires teamwork. Whether you are the CEO, manager of a department or an employee you are part of a team. Your company has smart people working there, and it's natural that not everyone agrees with everything. You probably even disagree with some things at your company over which you may not have total control. The CEO, who presumably has influence over everything at the company, knows that getting everyone in the company to believe in the mission, understand the strategies, and effectively work together to

[45] Michael Shevack, The Six Fix, Spiritual Healthcare for a Stronger America, Enlightened Religion Press, 2023.

achieve the company's objectives is, itself, a challenge.

Regardless of your position on the team, your obligation is to help the team succeed. A business is essentially a team, and a combination of smaller teams. All need to work together for the common good. When a business is successful it's better for everyone in that business.

If you truly are not able to get behind the mission at your company; if you cannot find motivation within your present company; you have a particular problem. It might be time to find another team.

Be good to your team. Be a good team member, regardless of your role on the team.

All businesses need to replenish themselves. New generations of employees and leaders need to be recruited and trained. Handing off authority can be difficult. Again, the new manager likely will have somewhat different ideas from yourself. But this is part of the business growing.

Your business also must be good for "All Life and Creation". If your business is wasting natural resources or polluting natural areas that needs to take priority for improvement. And, let's face it, no process, including any business process, is perfect. All processes use natural resources in some way, and all processes have outcomes that are wasteful, possibly harmful.

You may be in a business that heavily utilizes natural resources. The industry in which you work may have contributed substantially to worldwide pollution. For example, suppose you work for an oil company, a mining company, or a plastics manufacturer. Indeed, your industry has contributed significantly to raising human standards of living. And no doubt, it is very difficult to change the course of a company, let alone an industry, in a short time. Nevertheless, you are obligated to improve, and you should work hard to become part of the solution to societal pollution challenges.

This gets us to the last, but perhaps most important, priority: Continue to improve.

Only *God* is perfect. Our human purpose is to make the world a better place. So, too, must our businesses, which are just an extension of ourselves, work to make the world a better place.

Miracles - Be Alert

In our business planning we set priorities, logical steps that lead to successful attainment of our business goals. But often the unexpected occurs, and sometimes that occurrence is a spiritual signal that should not be ignored.

> *And the angel of the Lord appeared to him in a flame of fire out of the midst of a bush; and he looked, and lo, the bush was burning, yet it was not consumed.*
>
> \- *Exodus 3:2*

Miracles in business are real. Jews expect them, though, we never rely on them.

> *One should never put himself in a dangerous situation and say, "A miracle will save me". Perhaps the miracle will not come. And even if a miracle occurs, one's merits are reduced.*
>
> \- *Talmud*

Every spiritually open businessperson has noticed strange curiosities and synchronicities. Businesspeople receive unexpected sales opportunities, make new important business acquaintances, or suddenly experience unique business opportunities. And these happen in astonishing ways.

Jews call these experiences *b'shert,* which is *Yiddish* for "destiny". Perhaps these occurrences are coincidences, purely random. No matter, such occurrences can be great opportunities.

B'shert happens in our everyday lives, as well as in business. Meeting the man or woman whom we marry and who becomes our lifelong partner is often called *b'shert.*

Be alert and recognize *b'shert* in your business when it happens. Take advantage of it. Don't let your rational mind prevent you from marveling at the seemingly random goodness of it.

This is b*usiness spirituality*. These seemingly random occurrences are *God*-sent business opportunities to help you achieve.

> *Then the Lord said: "I am making a covenant with you. Before all your people I will do wonders never before done in any nation in all the world. The people you live among will see how awesome is the work that I, the LORD, will do for you.*
>
> *- Exodus 34:10*

"*God* doesn't expect a reward". The only expectation is that you do what is good and right.

We find it hard to accept miracles. We've been educated to expect science ultimately to explain everything about the universe, and we've lived to experience almost unbelievable advances in science and technology. As a result, we tend to see a dichotomy between science and *God*, but the dichotomy is exaggerated and misses the point.

Einstein, a secular Jew himself, said:

> *There are two ways to live. You can live as if nothing is a miracle; you can live as if everything is a miracle.*

The more we learn the more we appreciate what we don't know. *God*'s Creation is bigger and more unfathomable than humankind may ever fully understand.

We've learned that the universe is built with uncertainty integral within it[46].

We also know, as Darwin discovered, that evolution is integral to how nature goes forward. Evolution is the slow but sure way that nature adapts to changing environments through mutations that are random and that get selected for continuance only if they provide a benefit to life.

---

[46] Heisenberg wrote in 1927 what came to be called "Heisenberg's Uncertainty Principle".

The wise Jew accepts uncertainty.

Jews don't blame *God* when bad things happen. When a Jew dies the prayer that is said at every funeral is *Psalm* 23, which begins "The Lord is my Shepard." It is a prayer that praises *God.*

We know that sometimes bad things happen to good people, like disease and accidents. And who hasn't felt disappointed when we've tried to do our best, but we didn't see the immediate results we expected.

While uncertainty sometimes leads to disappointing results, we wouldn't want, nor could we imagine Life, that didn't have uncertainty. We cherish the freedom of self-determination. We just try harder.

Unexplainable events also are often positive. Things seem to go our way. Some would call this *luck*.

Others would call it *destiny,* or *God*'s Will. Jews, in *Yiddish*, call this, *b'shert.*

Traditions – Inherited Knowledge

> *Because of our traditions, we've kept our balance for many, many years.*
>
> - Sheldon Harnick and Jerry Bock[47]

Judaism evolved throughout the ages, and there are many Jewish laws and traditions.

[47] "Fiddler on the Roof", 1964 Broadway show, Sheldon Harnick and Jerry Bock, Jewish lyricist and composer

Some Jewish laws derive from specific verses in *Torah.* Keeping Sabbath, which is the fourth commandment, is an example.

> *Remember the Sabbath by keeping it holy.*
>
> \- *Exodus* 20:8

Much of Jewish law comes from *Talmud, a* major part of which was compiled between 300 to 500 CE. These sections of *Talmud* are organized into sections pertaining to:

Prayer and agricultural laws

Sabbath, holiday laws, and mourning regulations.

Rules pertaining to marriage and divorce.

Money matters.

Dietary laws.

Ritual purity and family purity.

Various Jewish denominations (e.g. Orthodoxy, Conservative, Reform, Reconstruction, Renewal) interpret some of these laws differently.

"Traditions" are different than "laws". Many Jewish traditions have been adapted based upon local and familial customs.

> For example, in many families, mine included, on *Rosh Hashanah,* which is the Jewish New Year, our tradition is to eat apples with honey as a symbol of sweetness and yearning for a new, sweet year. This is a nice tradition. Its symbolism has meaning, but it is not a religious law.

All Jews would agree that traditions add richness and value to our lives. They especially have become embedded in holiday observances and life cycle events.

All religions have their own traditions, and we must respect the rights of others to enjoy and celebrate their own heritage.

Businesses, too, have "laws" and "traditions". Every business must obey the law of the nations in which they do business. *Talmud* requires Jews to be law-abiding citizens of whatever country they find themselves in.

Business traditions can be more idiosyncratic to each business or even to a business location. For example:

> Business dress codes vary. Titles vary.
>
> The manager of a business location dismisses work early the last Friday of the month when their location meets their numbers for the month.
>
> Staff meetings frequency, time, and attendees vary.
>
> Larger group meetings may be regular occurrences to disseminate information or for team development.

The wise business leader respects the traditions practiced historically in their industry, business, and location. He or she cultivates meaningful business traditions that add meaning and joy for their teams.

Put It To Work

Asah (Do)

- At work, if you are in a situation in which you are morally uncomfortable don't just go along. At minimum, talk to your supervisor or manager about your perception. If still not satisfied, seek outside confidential advice from your family members and/ or clergy.
- Be observant of the miracles that occur each day and each season.
- Be good to yourself. Be good to others.

Bara (Create)

- Whenever you face a tough problem, ask yourself, "What would God want me to do?" It doesn't matter what your concept of God is, or even if you don't believe in God per se, ask yourself this question anyway.

- Be alert and open-minded to recognize b'shert in your own life. Whether or not you accept that it "was meant to be", thank God. When these occurrences happen, use the positive energy to do even more good.

- Don't lose sight of traditions. There is underlying wisdom in almost all traditions. Why did a particular tradition arise? Is that still meaningful today? How could we make a tradition more meaningful and relevant to today?

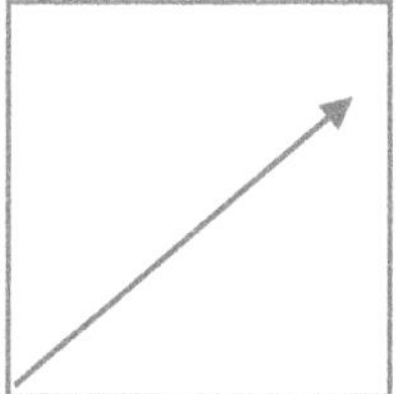

Man Plans and God Laughs[48]

Moses warned the Hebrews "not to act wickedly" and not to make sculptured images. He goes on:

> *And when you look up to the sky and see the sun, the moon and the stars—all the heavenly array—do not be enticed into bowing down to them and worshiping things the Lord your God has apportioned to all the nations under heaven.*
>
> \- *Deuteronomy* 4:19

As tempting as these images may be, they are false idols. Even the heavens, as awesome as they are, were created by *God*; they are not *God.*

We face tempting diversions throughout our lives, including of course in business. Promises of quick riches or a quick fix are like idols. Beware of false promises.

Jewish Nobel prize-winning economist Milton Friedman was fond of saying, "There is no such thing as a free lunch." The acronym, *TANSTAAFL*[49] is a very valuable business lesson. When something appears to be too good to be true, beware! It most likely is not true.

---

48 *Yiddish* saying

49 Edwin Dolan, TANSTAAFL, 1971. This phrase also can be traced to the late 19th century when bars offered "free lunch" with the purchase of a drink, with the notion that a salty lunch would induce buying more drinks.

Fools Get Fooled

In business there are no buddies.

\- *Yiddish* Proverb

In your business career, no matter your position, you will be confronted by opportunities that are enticing. How do you recognize what is truly a good opportunity versus a fly-by-night scheme.

> A lot of new restaurants fail in their first year of operation[50]. Obviously, every one of these restaurant entrepreneurs predicted that their restaurant venture would succeed.
>
> Venture capitalists, who invest in startup businesses, sometimes admit that less than 10% of their investments turn out well[51]. They hope the few investments that are profitable more than make up for their losers.

Surely, you want to listen to new opportunities, and you want to get in on the next new thing. Let's even presume that the salespeople, those who are pitching the new idea to you, mean well. They should believe in the opportunity they are selling.

Keep this acronym in mind: "*TANSTAAFL*". ("There ain't no such thing as a free lunch"). There are many, perhaps most, new ideas that fail, despite good intentions.

Due diligence is required. Understand the costs. Investigate what may go wrong. Don't be blinded by promises of quick riches. Don't get rushed into what may be career-altering decisions for you.

In your due diligence try to answer these types of questions:

> Is there science behind it?
>
> Is there good market research, backed up by statistics, that indicates customer demand will be strong for this new product?

---

[50] National Restaurant Association estimates the failure rate for new restaurants to be 30%. A 2005 study by Ohio State University estimated the failure rate to be as high as 90%. (foodindustry.com)

[51] Marc Andreesen, founding partner of Venture Capital Firm Andreesen Horowitz (Corporate Finance Institute, June 15, 2023)

Is the management competent?

Who is the competition, and where are they in this race to market?

Are the costs well understood?

Is the supply chain manageable? Can the new venture ramp up production sufficiently if the demand is there?

What else could go wrong?

TANSTAAFL is a warning sign. It doesn't mean never do the venture. It warns you to do your homework.

Trends and Head Fakes

Those who have succeeded at anything and don't mention luck are kidding themselves.

- Larry King[52]

When something repeats itself, we tend to believe it. Our natural human inclination is to expect a repeating phenomenon to keep recurring.

Will the sun come up tomorrow? Well, the sun has been coming up every morning throughout our lives. So, sure, the sun will come up tomorrow. It may be cloudy, but even so night will turn into day.

At the casino roulette table, you see a string of black numbers. Will the next one be black? You know that the string of blacks is just a random occurrence, but you'll bet on black anyway. Or perhaps you'll bet on red, since you figure that over the long run there will be an equal number of blacks and red, so perhaps red is due.

These examples represent the extremes. Sunrise is a sure thing. We understand that the earth revolves on its axis, and daylight occurs on the side of the earth facing the sun. Roulette is different. Reds and blacks are evenly divided in roulette, and each spin is independent of what came

---

[52] Larry King was a much-awarded radio and television host. His parents were Orthodox Jews who escaped prejudice and persecution in Belarus by emigrating to the U.S. in the 1920's.

before.[53]

But many sequences are not so easy to predict. Consider this baseball example:

> Slugger hit 40 home runs last year. This year, at the All-Star break, which is halfway through this season, Slugger hit 25 home runs so far. How many home runs will Slugger hit for this whole season?
>
> It's logical to project 50, 40, or 45 home runs. If Slugger hits the same number of home runs in the second half of the season as in the first half, his total will be 50 home runs for this whole season. If Slugger reverts to his average performance he will hit 40 home runs, same as last year. Or we could project 20 for the second half of the season, one-half of his average performance, plus the 25 home runs already hit in the first half.

Data sequences are measured in essentially all fields of endeavor, and analysts in those fields are challenged to make educated guesses about what will happen in the near future. This happens in sports, weather, politics, education, science and business - in all areas of study.

A "trend" is a pattern that we notice in a sequence. When we see repetition in a result or a continual rate of change, we tend to predict that the trend will continue.

But, sometimes, it's a "head fake". A "head fake" is a basketball term; the player with the ball moves his head one way while his legs take the ball the opposite way fooling the defending player.

It can be very difficult to ascertain whether a true trend is developing. For the companies or institutions involved in these types of decisions, predicting whether a trend will continue can be very significant. Consider these business examples:

> Average prices are increasing but not increasing as much as they had been. Should the U.S. Federal Reserve keep interest rates the same

[53] A wise guy might say that billions of years from now our sun will burn out, and so there will be no morning. And the wise guy might say that perhaps the roulette table is fixed or broken in some way, so that the odds of reds versus blacks are not equal.

> to control inflation, or reduce interest rates?
>
> Sales of diet drinks have been increasing more than for non-diet drinks. Should the soft drink company switch their production to make relatively more diet drinks?
>
> People have been buying more expensive smart phones. Should the smart phone company produce less of their inexpensive smart phones? Should they reduce the price of their inexpensive smart phones to stimulate sales? Should they increase the price of the expensive versions to generate more profits?

How do you decide if an apparent trend will continue? The answer is, "You really don't know". Various analysts may differ.

Analysts will hypothesize what might be the cause of the apparent trend, and they'll investigate to try to validate that potential cause. Conversely, if there is no explanation for the trend, they'll lean towards assuming it's random.

Timeframes also are a key consideration. Has the trend been apparent for a long time, or has the apparent trend suddenly appeared? The longer a trend has been happening it usually indicates that it's more likely to continue.

The problem with waiting to see if a trend continues, of course, is that if the trend is real then critical time to react to the trend will have been lost.

Statistics is a branch of mathematics that puts probabilities on things based upon what past observations show. Computer modeling combined with statistics may be utilized to help forecast trends. For example:

> A hurricane is forming in the Caribbean Sea. Based upon past models (computer simulations) the U.S. Weather Service predicts that the hurricane is tracking towards the coast of Florida. The landfall is predicted to be between Miami and Ft. Lauderdale.

Some trends are well accepted, and businesses are reacting to benefit as these trends unfold. Demand is shifting for some major industries, which are likely to have wide ranging impacts.

Electric Vehicles (BEV) are expected to capture an increasing proportion of majority of vehicle sales in a few years.

Health services are changing rapidly due to scientific breakthroughs as well as demographic shifts.

Artificial Intelligence (AI) is advancing rapidly will impact almost all industries over the next decade or so.

Business fortunes are won, or lost, because of forecasting trends and spotting true turning points.

Years ago, we were members of a synagogue that held their High Holiday services at a hotel. When *Rosh Hashanah*, the initial holiday among the "High Holy Days", services were over it was close to lunch time. The congregants leaving services headed to the restaurant at the hotel, and the hotel restaurant was over-whelmed by the number of customers.

The following week the restaurant manager planned. He stocked more food and had more staff on hand ten days later on *Yom Kippur*, Hebrew for "Day of Atonement".

What happened? Nobody went to that restaurant when services took a recess at midday on *Yom Kippur*. (The *Yom Kippur* tradition is to fast for that day.)

It's a funny story, but it wasn't funny for the manager of that restaurant. He didn't understand his customers, and consequently he grossly misjudged the demand for his product.

Trends occur on the macro level, and they also may occur within your own business, your own store.

Try to understand what is causing an apparent trend, so that you don't get fooled by a "head fake".

There Are Always Hidden Costs

The key traits that lead to wasteful behavior are anger, pride, and most of all, ego. To tread lightly and live without wasting, one must cultivate the opposite of these traits - inner peace, humility, and selflessness.

- Rabbi Samson Raphael Hirsh[54]

God tells the Hebrews, via Moses, that their land will provide for them, and they will dwell in their land securely. Economics, at the time, was almost totally agrarian, so this guarantee was a big deal.

But notice that *God* demanded a *quid pro quo*. The Hebrews had to follow *God*'s laws and faithfully observe *God*'s commandments.

Nothing is for nothing. There is always a *quid pro quo*. Even when an opportunity turns out to be a winner it almost always comes at a cost - significant work effort, shutting out other opportunities, capital investment, etc.

Every process has imperfections. Nothing is perfect. In business, we see that everything involves costs.

The flip side of this limitation is an opportunity. Everything can be improved.

> Part of our fascination with sports is that athletes seem to continually break records. At one time it was thought impossible that a person could run a mile in under four minutes[55]. Babe Ruth hit 40 home runs in one baseball season, thought to be an unbeatable record at the time, yet Barry Bonds hit 72 home runs in 2001. Mark Spitz became famous in 1972 for winning seven gold medals at the Olympics; his record was surpassed by Michael Phelps_who won eight gold medals at the 2004 Olympics.

Businesses utilize Key Performance Indicators (KPIs) to measure how well their processes are performing. An important KPI is the percentage

---

[54] Rabbi Hirsh (1808-1888) was one of the leaders in Germany for the Modern Orthodox movement.

[55] Roger Bannister ran the mile in 3 minutes and 59.4 seconds in 1954.

of products that come off a manufacturer's assembly line that fails to meet their inspection standards. Astute manufacturers measure this KPI and continually improve their processes to lower that output failure rate.

Continuous improvement applies to both the internal and external processes in your business, although it's easier for businesses to concern themselves with resources and processes within the confines of their business.

It's important, though, that businesses also concern themselves with how they impact the environment. Environmental impacts are harder to measure, but environmental costs are nevertheless real.

Work is a privilege bestowed by *God*, and we are obligated to consider costs, however indirect, to society.

Put It To Work

Asah (Do)

- You will be presented with many opportunities. You cannot pursue all of them. Be choosey.

- Do your due diligence before you invest much of your time or any of your money.

- When something looks too good to be true, assume it isn't true. Or, at least, don't bet too much on it.

Bara (Create)

- Stay abreast of current events and worldwide economic trends. Look for opportunities where the general market hasn't priced in likely future events. But be careful. The markets usually are efficient, meaning that the market generally already sees what you see.

- Diagnose the cause of any apparent trend. If you cannot explain why the trend has happened assume you are looking at randomness, rather than a true trend. History doesn't always repeat itself.

- Don't just measure tangible costs. Intangible costs are important to consider, too. If a decision or investment doesn't feel good to you, then it isn't good for you.

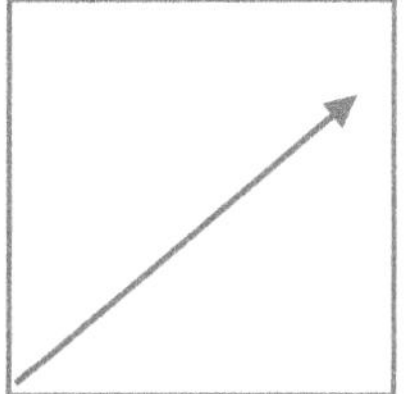

Part 3 – Business Practicum

Find Your Place

Some time later God tested Abraham. He said to him, "Abraham!" "Here I am," he replied.

- *Genesis* 22:1

So said Abraham in response to *God*'s call to him. Jacob and Moses similarly replied to *God*.

The Hebrew "*Hineni*" is a conjunction of two Hebrew words meaning "Here" and "I", but it is more emphatic than just saying "Here am I". *Hineni* affirmed they were ready to respond to *God*'s call to action, without pre-conditions and without knowing all that would be required.

"It is the kind of response we offer only a few times in our lives: When we promise ourselves to the one we love not knowing what the future might bring; when we gaze into a newborn's eyes and promise we will never let them down; when we promise ourselves – as we enter a new era of our lives - to be all that we can be."[56]

Your job has this kind of significance for you. When you take a job, you don't know all that will be required of you. You are committing to be all that you can be for yourself, for your workmates, for your employer - and for your customers.

Work is a huge part of your adult life. You won't be happy in your life if you don't enjoy your work. To enjoy your work, you must believe in what you are doing.

How do you find your own inspiration? How do you choose and develop your own path?

[56] sefaria.org "The Deepest Meanings of *Hineni*"

Know Yourself

> *Be rather a tail to lions than a head to foxes. Be rather a humble member of an eminent company than associate with inferiors in order to stand out prominently amongst them.*
>
> *- Talmud*

Whatever you do, if you do it well that is good.

Ambition is all about setting high goals for yourself and working hard towards achieving those goals. For yourself! You want to do well for your family, of course, but you must be true to yourself first.

Understand your own capabilities. What do you like to do? People usually like doing what they are good at.

One mentor told me "Work should be fun." And it is fun if you feel that you are making progress and doing good in the world. This happens when your job leverages your skills, and you feel challenged but capable of achieving meaningful goals.

Look for a job situation where you'll be doing what you love. There are many fields of endeavor, and no one field of work is inherently better or even necessarily more lucrative than others.

> *The Holy One, blessed be he, makes every occupation agreeable in the eyes of those who follow it.*
>
> *- Talmud*

Think big and think at least two steps ahead. What will come after you achieve the immediate goal that you are setting for yourself? Envision your goals in timeframes. For example, what do I want to accomplish this year? And where do I envision myself in three years?

Be realistic. Be comfortable with where you currently are in your career. You may be in school preparing for a career. You may be just starting out, or you may be a mid-level manager. Or, you may be more advanced, running a project, department, or have even broader business responsibilities.

Your personal business plan is for your own benefit. Not everyone wants to be in management or run their own business. What do you want for yourself? Whatever your goal, envisioning it for yourself will make you a better employee, colleague, and business teammate.

Some people get lucky. They readily find a good business fit for themselves. They seem to know exactly what they want their career to be. They seem to be in the right place at the right time. That is *b'shert,* or destiny.

But it's no surprise and nothing to be ashamed of if finding the right workplace for yourself takes time. There are a lot of complexities that need to fit together for you. You must have the skills to do the job. You must be able to work well with your teammates and your manager. Your teammates will change, as people rotate within the company or leave the company. When you are ready for a promotion or a new opportunity the exact next right situation for you may or may not be available.

Everyone, at every level in business, has customers and stakeholders. These are the people you must please to succeed. Hopefully, their goals are reasonably consistent with yours. But other people won't see the world exactly as you do, and that, too, is to be expected.

Be adaptable. Nothing is perfect, and everything can be improved.

Only you can set goals for yourself and motivate yourself towards those goals.

You are unique. Whatever you do, if you do it well and you believe you are doing good you will be successful.

Get Inspired

> *One of the goals of the Jewish way of living is to experience commonplace deeds as spiritual adventures, to feel the hidden love and wisdom in all things.*
>
> \- *Heschel*, a noted 20th century rabbi[57]

[57] Abraham Joshua Heschel, God in Search of Man; A Philosophy of Judaism, Harper and Row, January 1966

Kabbalah teaches that we deal with the world in four realms: doing, feeling, thinking, and being.

> At one level we do things. We go to work. We read our emails. We buy raw materials. We answer customers' questions. Our actions should feel inspiring, because we should recognize how our actions lead to doing good.
>
> Second, we feel things. We get feedback from the world from what we do. It makes us happy or sad, tired or exhilarated. We share our feelings with our teammates, since business successes or failures affect the team. Sense how a business situation is affecting your teammates and be aware how your own actions affect others. If animals are involved in your business, try to sense what they might be feeling. Feelings are contagious.
>
> Third, we think. How could I have done this better? What caused me to feel happy? How should I adjust my activities in the future to do more good?
>
> The highest level is spirituality. Jews aspire to connect spiritually to *God* for inspiration. What is good is what *God* would want us to do. How do we connect with *God*? We meditate. We pray. We don't ask *God* for things. Rather, we ask ourselves whether we are doing what God would want us to do.

So, yes, our work may seem commonplace at times. Sometimes it feels like drudgery to get up and go to work. *Doing* the work, though, is part of the whole experience of working. See the connections among *doing*, *feeling*, *thinking* and *spirituality* to make your work more satisfying for you.

Jewish wisdom helps us to elevate our work, to be more spiritual, and in so doing helps us to work better.

Avodah, in Hebrew, means "work". It also means "worship". When we engage in any enterprise, we are connecting to *God*'s enterprise. When we do business like a Jew, we acknowledge this obvious existential fact, and put mere money-making in perspective.

Acknowledge, at least to yourself, that you are doing "avodah". Knowing that you are worshipping *God* by doing Good is spiritually uplifting. You will feel more purposeful, more motivated, and your business decisions will become clearer for you. You will enjoy your work more.

Now, your *work* is a true sacrifice, *avodah,* service to *God.*

Set Worthy Goals

> *When Moses sent them to explore Canaan, he said, "Go up through the Negev and on into the hill country. See what the land is like and whether the people who live there are strong or weak, few or many.*
>
> \- *Numbers* 13:17-18; 25-28

Moses declared a decisive goal to lead his people, and he utilized his scouts to make a more informed decision about how to achieve that goal.

Moses knew Canaan was the goal, because *God* had directed him to lead the Israelites there. Moses was so connected spiritually with *God* that he didn't question whether Canaan was a worthy goal? And he didn't hesitate in the face of what may have seemed a daunting task.

Nevertheless, Moses sent scouts. We can surmise that he wanted more information to plan his tactics for the final entry into Canaan. Perhaps he also was testing the resolve of his scouting party.

We're not Moses, but we set goals for ourselves and plan our tactics to reach our goals all the time. Some of our goals are short-term and relatively trivial, and some goals are long-term and guide our actions over months or even years.

Free will! We influence the future by what we do today. Other people influence us, and we influence them, both at home and at work. Also, seemingly random things occur that cause us to reevaluate and alter our plans.

How do we reconcile the myriad of influences and decide what to do? We implicitly ask ourselves three practical questions:

"Is this goal worth the effort?"

"Is this goal worth the risk?"

> "Among the infinite things that I could be doing, is this the goal that should get my attention and priority?"

Everything takes effort, and everything has risk. That is part of the reality of our world that we observe and study in Physics.

Since we cannot do everything, when we set a specific goal, we're also deciding what we're not going to do. Obviously, we don't want to pursue anything bad. Bad alternatives are usually easy to rule out, but sometimes side effects of our actions are unforeseen. Sometimes we start towards a goal with good intentions, and we learn along the way about some previously unforeseen impacts.

We also want to set ambitious goals. Teachers know that setting relatively high goals for their students leads their students to achieve more. The same goes for sports coaches; athletes push themselves to break their previous records.

Business goals should be ambitious to achieve optimum effort, but not so high that that the goal seems unattainable. This leads to a common paradox. Employees and work teams hate to fail. But, if a goal is truly challenging, then it won't be achieved 100% of the time.

How do we know our goals are worthy? We ask ourselves, "Would *God* consider this worthy?"

Be Diligent

> *The Lord God took the man and put him in the Garden of Eden to work it and take care of it.*
>
> - *Genesis* 2:15

From the very beginning Adam had a job, even in the garden of Eden. He was the gardener.

> *Then the eyes of both of them were opened, and they realized they were naked; so they sewed fig leaves together and made coverings for themselves.*
>
> - *Genesis* 3-7

We previously discussed how Adam and Eve learned about good and evil. The other profound lesson was that they had to work to provide for themselves.

What did Adam and Eve do right away? They invented clothing. Out in the world, outside of Eden, humans need protection. We take clothing for granted, but clothing was a brilliant invention. Only humans invent, manufacture, and utilize clothing to enable us to survive in environments that are not ideal.

We invent things to make life better, to make the world a better place. We couldn't survive without protective clothing. We have countless other inventions that enable us to survive and prosper.

Businesses are an invention, too. Humans learned to work together to get their work done better. Way before Abraham, pre-historic men learned to hunt together, and by doing so they were able to kill larger prey. Agriculture was a leap forward for humanity requiring planning throughout the year for planting and harvesting. Obviously, modern businesses are often much bigger and more complex, with multiple locations, specialized professions, and connections to many other businesses for supplies, distribution, outsourcing, etc.

For those of us who have had experiences working within a large company we know that there are always personnel issues — problems finding and recruiting the right people, problems motivating people, dealing with poor performance problems.

Getting everyone in the business to "row in the same direction" is a big part of management's responsibility. Motivating other people is every manager's job, not just the CEO. This takes leadership, good communications, and hard work.

Expect problems. Planning the work; motivating others to help do the work; and making necessary mid-course corrections gets complicated. There are always tradeoffs and choices.

Work requires continually balancing the myriad of influences, so that you and your team achieve the objectives that you've set for yourself and with your team.

Heigh Ho, Heigh Ho, It's Home From Work We Go[58]

Remember the sabbath day by keeping it holy.

- *Exodus* 20:8

The Hebrews were slaves in Egypt where work for them was all consuming. *God* brought them out from Egypt to Mt. Sinai, where Moses ascended to the mountaintop to receive the Ten Commandments from *God.* Keeping the Sabbath is the Fourth Commandment.

Shabbat is Hebrew for "sabbath". Jews celebrate S*habbat* on the seventh day of the week and consider *Shabbat* to be the holiest of Jewish holidays. On *Shabbat* Jews are not supposed to work, and religious Jews follow this *mitzvah,* commandment, strictly.

Sabbath was a Jewish invention. This Jewish insight to separate yourself from work at the end of each week is now accepted by almost all cultures as being beneficial to human welfare and to increased productivity. This Jewish innovation took courage, since in ancient times the Greeks and Romans accused the Jews of being lazy.

Judaism's wisdom regarding sabbath goes beyond rest. It is a time to reconnect and recharge our spiritual energy.

Keeping *Shabbat* holy requires a consciousness shift. It is not meant to be simply a day off. Jewish wisdom teaches that each of us has a direct connection to *God*, but it is up to each of us to spiritually engage with *God.* On *Shabbat* we pause to honor *God*, thank *God*, and pray and study so that we do more Good going forward.

The lessons of *Shabbat* also provide meaning and guidance for us during the rest of the week. It's inevitable that our family lives and our work lives get blended. We need to recognize the importance of separation between our family life and our work life, or both may suffer.

In the animated Disney movie, *Snow White*, the seven dwarves sang the lyric "Heigh ho, heigh ho, it's home from work we go". They were glad

---

[58] Larry Morey, "Heigh Ho Heigh Ho" from Disney film: Snow White and the Seven Dwarfs. Morey, a Jewish lyricist, wrote many songs for Disney.

to leave work, to get back to Snow White. (A lot of us mistakenly sing, "Heigh ho, heigh ho, it's off to work we go". But that is not the actual lyric. It seems, we're trained to over-emphasize working.)

It's inevitable that our family life and our work life get blended. However, how we blend them and weight them is often our choice.

Our family life comes with us when we go to work, usually in an incidental way but sometimes intrusively. We intentionally bring reminders of our family life to our workplace. We place photos of our family on or near our desks. We brag about our kids to our co-workers on our lunch breaks. During our workday we cram in personal errands or phone calls to take care of family matters. If we have a sick family member at home or some other family crisis, we carry those concerns with us all day.

Similarly, we take our work concerns home with us. We like to discuss work victories, such as a big sale or a promotion, with our spouse. When we're very busy we bring the work home to do after dinner or on the weekend.

Today, modern communications and computerization have made it feasible to work virtually. We can work from home or from anywhere. Cell phones connect us to our work 24x7.

Jewish wisdom invented *Shabbat*, because we recognized the importance of unplugging from work. "Unplugging" figuratively in the olden days, and "unplugging" literally today.

God rested on the seventh day. Humans rest on *Shabbat*, the seventh day of every week.

Jewish wisdom also teaches us that even the land used for farming needs to rest every seventh year to rejuvenate.

> *Speak to the Israelites and say to them: 'When you enter the land I am going to give you, the land itself must observe a sabbath to the Lord."*
>
> \- *Leviticus* 25:2

Shmita[59] is the Jewish agricultural practice of observing a sabbatical year, a sabbath, for farmland. Farmland is not to be farmed every seventh year, letting the land replenish itself.

Taking a sabbatical has spread to academics and clergy. These professionals feed us with knowledge, just as the land feeds us food. During their sabbatical academics and clergy are supposed to study and refresh their knowledge.

Most businesses close at least one day per week. Some businesses, like hospitals, need to maintain continuous operations, but nevertheless their employees need to rest. Besides giving staff a day off, the medical profession has realized that doctors in training cannot be expected to work undue hours continuously in a safe and effective manner.

All business inputs are ultimately gifts from *God*. We honor *God* when we give all our employees and ourselves, as well as all the natural resources that our business utilizes a rest.

We say, *Shabbat Shalom.* That is a Hebrew expression which translates to English as "sabbath peace". May you, your work team, and all the resources upon which we depend enjoy sabbath peace.

Listen While You Pray

> *"We need fewer words and more room for silence. We need fewer prayers and more time for reflection."*
>
> \- Daniel Matt[60]

There is ancient wisdom buried in Jewish prayer practices, even if you don't participate in formal Jewish prayer ritual. In fact, even for Jews

---

[59] *Shmita* is usually not strictly practiced today but is honored spiritually in several ways. For example, In Israel food that grows without farming intervention during the sabbatical year is free for Israelis to harvest for themselves. Some farmers in Israel sell their land to the rabbinic court for the sabbatical year so that proceeds from the produce is given to charity.

[60] Daniel Matt, PhD , God and the Big Bang: Discovering Harmony Between Science and Spirituality, Jewish Lights Publishing, April 2016.

who do routinely participate in Jewish ritual services this wisdom will guide you to find inspiration.

The key is "listen"! Creative inspirations pop into your consciousness. It's like the old cartoon showing a light bulb above your head. Light is symbolic of *God*, as if *God* "gave" you the inspiration.

In Jewish minds, *God* is the creator of everything, including our inspirations. Jewish prayer is intended to help us find inspiration.

Jewish prayer follows a set order. In the middle of every service is the *Shema* which begins with a key statement:

Hear of Israel, the Lord is our God, the Lord is One.

The *Shema* is often called the "watchword of our faith". "*Shema*" is Hebrew meaning "hear". You must open your ears and your mind to really hear. *Shema* declares that there is one *God.*

Immediately after the *Shema* is the *Amidah,* a collection of 19 blessings. *Amidah* means "stand", as we stand during this prayer in deference to *God.* Jewish tradition requires that a group be present for the *Amidah.* The group starts together, but then each person proceeds silently at their own pace. The group finishes when the last person sits down. Spiritually, Jews recognize the importance of the group, but also that each Jew has their own connection with *God.*

Some rabbis tell their congregations that during the *Amidah*, a congregant may either recite the blessings as written in the prayerbook or meditate on their own. The key is that we don't want to recite the words so habitually that we don't concentrate and connect with the spiritual meaning.

When the mind is not so busy with day-to-day thoughts, there is space for an unconscious thought to become conscious, which can be a valuable inspiration.

Some people get inspiration as they are dreaming. When they are asleep, or in near sleep, sub-conscious thoughts become conscious.

Torah describes Moses' inspirational moment.

> *There the angel of the Lord appeared to him in flames of fire from within a bush. Moses saw that though the bush was on fire it did not burn up. So Moses thought, "I will go over and see this strange sight—why the bush does not burn up." When the Lord saw that he had gone over to look, God called to him from within the bush, "Moses! Moses!" And Moses said, "Here I am."*

- *Exodus* 3:2-4

The prophet Elijah heard *God* as a soft murmuring sound.

> *The Lord said, "Go out and stand on the mountain in the presence of the Lord, for the Lord is about to pass by." Then a great and powerful wind tore the mountains apart and shattered the rocks before the Lord, but the Lord was not in the wind. After the wind there was an earthquake, but the Lord was not in the earthquake. After the earthquake came a fire, but the Lord was not in the fire. And after the fire came a gentle whisper.When Elijah heard it, he pulled his cloak over his face and went out and stood at the mouth of the cave. Then a voice said to him, "What are you doing here, Elijah?"*

- *First Kings* 19:11-13

Great ideas often come as a still, soft voice from your unconscious.

All of us get inspirations. Not all inspirations are monumental, like Abraham's and Moses', but nonetheless can be very valuable.

Inspiration begins by listening. At least one purpose of praying is to still our minds so that we can think and listen to our own thoughts and, hopefully, be inspired.

Put It To Work

Asah (Do)

- Reflect deeply about what do you want to achieve in the next year? The next three years? Write your goals down.
- Get things done by working hard. Get the right things done by working intelligently.
- Separate from work on the sabbath.
- Give your teammates peace to separate from work on their sabbath.

Bara (Create)

- Connect what you are doing, feeling, and thinking with a spiritual sense that you are creating something good.
- Find a routine to be alone with your thoughts. In those moments try to shut out the noise of day-to-day tasks. Utilize meditative practices that work for you.
- Manage your work-life balance realistically. Both are important for the health of yourself, your family, and your business.
- Listen to inspirations. Write them down. Don't reject them out of hand.
- Modify your work plans over time as necessary.

Your Personal Promised Land

And God saw everything that he had made, and behold, it was very good. And there was evening and there was morning, a sixth day.

- *Genesis* 1:31

God created the world in steps. It took six days. At the end of each day, *God* reviewed what was accomplished so far.

You have your own vision. Your vision might contemplate something big and bold, like a new business venture. Or, your vision might contemplate a new career direction, which would be significant for you. Or, you might be manager of a department, and you envision ways to make your department significantly better.

Now what? How do you go about achieving your vision? What do you do first?

Before you start up a ladder, count the rungs.

- *Yiddish saying*

You need a plan. Your plan should set direction, define key steps to align efforts, and provide key measurable objectives to mark your progress.

Your vision will take longer than six days to accomplish. Most business plans span two, three, four or five years. Especially for the first year, you likely will want to plan interim periods, say quarterly. At convenient intervals you would take stock of your progress. You may declare, "That was good!" No matter what, take those opportunities to tweak your plan going forward.

Elevator Pitch

Start-up businesses generally need "seed" money to get started. "Angel Investors", as they are sometimes called, may provide you with that seed money. But make no mistake, Angel Investors expect to make a handsome profit in return for their investment. Angel Investors are typically shrewd experienced businesspeople, who receive requests from lots of entrepreneurs for seed money.

> "Shark Tank" is a popular TV show which portrays entrepreneurs hoping to obtain seed money for their business venture. The entrepreneurs have only a few minutes to make their pitch.

"Elevator Pitch" refers to the limited time an entrepreneur must entice an Angel Investor to give them seed money for their venture, whether it is on Shark Tank or anywhere else.

While this may seem impersonal, the fact is that you must be the champion for your new business venture. You need to be very clear about what your business would be, and you need to be able to explain the advantages of your product and your company's differentiation in a few minutes.

Even if you don't need to attract seed money to get started, it is a good idea to practice your elevator pitch. This forces you to have thought out clearly how your business will be good, or "value added".

Target Marketing

> *And God saw that the light was good; and God separated the light from the darkness.*
>
> \- *Genesis* 1:4

Marketing requires creativity. It also requires choices. It's very tempting to go after a wide swath of potential customers, because after all you envision becoming a big, successful business. But challenge yourself, especially in the early stages of your business, to define a relatively narrow target customer segment.

This will help you discover specific product benefits desired by that customer segment which will help you differentiate your offering. Your business also likely will learn repeatable skills to apply to your next target customer segment.

A narrower initial focus guides you and your team to gain specialized knowledge, which your potential customers will appreciate. Customers want to buy from an expert.

Also, be frank and honest about what you don't know and what your business doesn't do. Customers will appreciate this, too. Notice, for example, that professional firms, who essentially sell expertise, are becoming more and more specialized.

> Orthopedic surgeons, already requiring highly specialized training, tend to specialize further in knee replacement, hip replacement, hand surgery.
>
> Legal firms specialize in patent law, medical malpractice, securities law.
>
> Financial advisory firms specialize in fixed income investing, equity investing, commodities or international investing.

By targeting, or specializing, you send a message that you are experts in that area. And, by orienting everything in your company to focus on that particular area you would enhance that expertise.

Value Added

Do your target customers perceive a need for your product that is not currently met at all in the marketplace? Or does your vision entail convincing your target customers to switch from what they are buying today to your product? What does the competition not do well or not do at all that customers need?

Define your product's advantages. What is it about your product that is better? Will your target customers be wowed by your offering, or is your offering a more modest step above what the customers currently are getting?

Describe your product in as much detail as practical at this stage. Specifically, how would your product be better than the current competitions' product? How would your product work? Can you build a prototype?

If your product is a better replacement for what exists already in the marketplace collect price information for the current product offering. Does the current market price for the competing product set a ceiling on what you would charge? Would you need to price your product below the current market offering?

The marketplace will be attracted to real value-added products and services. You would advertise to raise awareness of the benefits of your product or service, but in the end customers will see and appreciate those benefits. Money flows towards value.

Getting Attention

Define your sales approach. What would grab the attention of your target customers?

If your product is very novel, how would you raise awareness among your potential customers that they need your product? This may sound strange, but many novel products don't immediately meet strong demand until early adopters set a style or pattern that others follow.

> Facebook was started in 2004 by Mark Zuckerberg to be an electronic yearbook at Harvard University. Demand for Facebook's capability surprised even Zuckerberg. Facebook quickly spread to other universities, and today is a giant social media company.

How do you intend to sell your product? Would you sell directly to end customers, or would you utilize an established sales intermediary? Are your target customers reachable via Internet, mail, or phone, or are face-to-face sales necessary?

For many products the sales process is a series of steps. A potential customer gets interested and gathers information. Hopefully, the potential customer's interest is piqued further. They may ask a friend their opinion. They may research your company and your product (or you) via social media. They may come back more than once, before they buy your product.

This doesn't end the sales process. The first time your customer utilizes your product is crucial. Based upon their initial experience with your product they may become a repeat customer, and hopefully a positive influencer for your product with other people. Obviously, you don't want your customer to be disappointed when they first try your product, but even if their experience doesn't go as well as you would hope you want to be prepared with customer service assistance and other follow-up.

Operations

At this point, you have a fairly good idea of your target customers, your product's value added, and a sales strategy. Think of this as your "Marketing Plan".

Now, you can define better how your company will accomplish fulfilling your marketing plan. How will the work get done? This is your "Operating Plan", which usually has three main components: Sales Operations, Manufacturing Operations, and Support Operations.

> Sales Operations: Salespeople and sales systems
>
> Manufacturing Operations: People, plant and equipment involved in making and delivering your product or service.
>
> Support Operations: Technology, Finance, Human Resources, and other Administration functions.

Various industries have different names for these various functions, but nevertheless essentially all businesses need to accomplish these types of functions.

If practical, identify existing companies that do similar things as you envision doing, and gather information about those companies. Besides scoping out the competition's product strengths and weaknesses, you likely will learn a lot about their operations.

List the various types of operations that your company would need and describe whether and how each would be a differentiator for your company. Not every operation has to be better than the competition, but some should be.

Would your company require specialized technology? Often, software packages are utilized that are tailored to a particular industry. Your business may also require specialized manufacturing machinery or require specialized skills. Identify such technologies and skills that you would require and whether these needed resources are readily available. Identify estimated costs to acquire and implement these technologies for your business.

Most companies outsource some of their functions, and outsourcing may be very practical for a startup enterprise. Outsourcing works well for functions which require large startup costs and for which differentiation is not especially critical.

Some support functions are necessary even though they are less customer facing. For example, someone needs to handle human resources. Someone must do the necessary accounting. Someone must take care of the company's physical location, including cleaning and maintenance. Many startups make the mistake of not planning enough for these support functions.

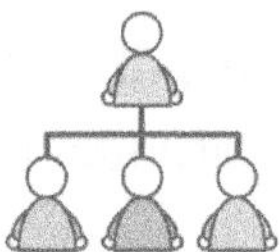

Organizing

There are many ways to organize your work teams, and over time it is likely that your internal organization will change. The numbers of people in your business likely will increase as your business grows. And you may want to change how you align responsibilities within your overall organization.

Business typically aligns management responsibilities in one or more of these approaches:

Functional alignment - Departments that specialize in a particular function.

Product center - The collection of functions involved in building and delivering a particular product.

Territorial - The people and their related functions that reside at a particular location.

Larger organizations typically organize utilizing a hybrid of these approaches.

There are tradeoffs to be considered. Functional alignment often is less expensive, because specialized talent is concentrated with a particular function. Product center or territorial alignment generally places your resources closer to where potential customers would be, and consequently tends to be better able to react to changing customer needs.

Your proposed organizational structure will define key management positions. If you have already identified some key people for these positions get them involved in helping to flesh out your business plan.

If you have not yet identified your key managers, how would you go about getting that talent into your company?

Financial Plan

Your financial plan puts it all together objectively. Your financial plan tests whether your business venture is likely to be successful and able to sustain itself.

This part of "Make Your Plan" involves some familiarity with financial concepts and spreadsheet tools. If you don't have this experience, seek assistance from a trusted advisor to help with this part of the planning.

Your projections should be realistic. You would hold yourself and your team accountable to meet the financial objectives portrayed in your financial plan. Your financial plan also may be provided to outside investors if your business venture requires outside funding, and those investors would expect you to meet the objectives inherent in the financial plan.

A key question is how quickly revenues would incept and how fast revenues would grow. Initially, there may not be any revenues as your business venture gets mobilized. Even after revenues begin to flow you usually would expect a period of time before revenues exceed expenses, and thus show a profit.

Estimate your revenues, how much would your business take in, based upon the amount of product you hope to sell and the expected price for your product.

Begin to estimate your costs. Usually, your costs would fall into three main categories, aligning with sales, manufacturing, and other operations. Develop your projected costs in each of these areas to reflect your approach in each of these areas.

> For example, if you plan to pay sales commissions then your projected sales costs might be reasonably estimated as a percentage of revenues.
>
> If your product requires raw materials, you might best estimate the material costs based upon the number of products sold and unit costs for the raw material.
>
> If you are outsourcing a particular operating function project costs for that function based upon the arrangement you have with that outsourcing vendor.

In any case, make sure that you contemplate expected costs for each operating function.

Calculate your bottom line. Revenues less Costs equals Net Income, or profit.

Finally, calculate a relative measure of profitability. There are various ways to portray relative profitability. Again, if this is not your area of expertise get suitable advice to develop your financial plan with you. Even if you are an expert in finance, it's best to get an advisor as a sounding board and to check your projections.

Test Your Plan

If you walk in my statutes and observe my commandments and do them, then I will give you your rains in their season, and the land shall yield its increase, and the trees of the field shall yield their fruit.

- *Leviticus* 26:3-4

The great Jewish scholar, Rashi [61], explains that "following" or "walking" in the ways of *God*'s statutes implies "toiling" in that effort. It takes work. You are not expected to understand *Torah* upon a first reading. You should go deeper. Engaging with the concepts and arguing them is part of the pathway to deeper understanding.

So, too, your business plan requires "toiling", testing it with others. That requires understanding it yourself, so that you can explain it clearly, simply, and efficiently to others.

You want to test your business plan especially with people who have knowledge of the business field in which you are endeavoring as well as other smart people who can constructively criticize your business plan. When you test your plan with others you will discover elements that you can improve, and how you can explain the benefits of your business better.

Watch and listen to your audiences. How excited is your audience? Are they interested? Is your differentiation compelling to them?

Don't be dismayed that you experience stage fright. After all, you've invested time and energy in developing your plan, and you don't want it to be rejected. You are a creative, hardworking, intelligent

[61] "Rashi" is an acronym for **Ra**bbi **S**chlomo **Y**itzhaki who lived in the 11th century.

businessperson, but you are not necessarily, nor do you have to be, the greatest salesperson. Your audience will mostly pick up on your excitement and energy and the clarity of your thinking.

Don't be surprised if initially your plan doesn't "wow" your first audiences. That is to be expected. That is all part of fine tuning your message. As you reflect on the difficulties of explaining your unique business approach you likely will discover ways to improve your plan and highlight your key points of differentiation.

The important point is "Test your plan"! Everything can be improved. Careful planning greatly increases your chances for success.

Put It To Work

Asah (Do)

- Write down your elevator pitch for your business venture. Be clear and concise.
- Research how many people would be in your target segment; where they are located; and whether that segment is growing.
- Develop a checklist of the main functions to be performed in your company.
- For each function describe specialized knowledge or tools needed.
- For each function describe what factors most contribute to costs.
- Draw a diagram of your organization chart.
- Identify the key management positions and list the name(s) of the individuals you have or would recruit for these positions.
- Get an advisor, if you need one, to help with building the spreadsheet to portray your financial plan.
- Carefully input the assumptions that drive your financial plan model.

- Practice presenting your business plan.

Bara (Create)

- Try out your elevator pitch on friends or trusted advisors. Do they think your business venture sounds very enticing?
- Define the market segment you initially want to target.
- Describe the characteristics of your product or service offering that you think will be very convincing to your target customers.
- What can and would you do to increase target customers awareness of your product?
- Review your plan with potential key managers, outsourcing partners, as well as investors in your company

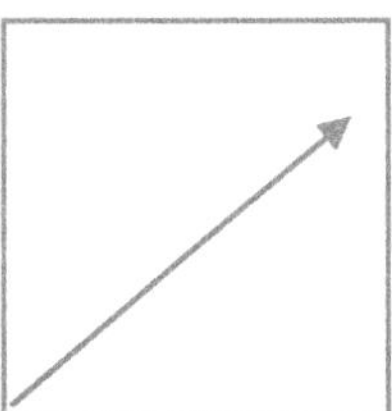

Knock Down The Walls

Praise be you God who commands us to busy ourselves with words of Torah.

- *Talmud*

Virtues such as humility, truthfulness, and helpfulness are universal ideals to which each of us aspires.

And yet, every person misses the mark, at least occasionally. Situations occur throughout our daily lives that require us to react in the moment. To be our best requires that we have a strong sense of values and the self-awareness to apply those values in our everyday interactions with other people including in our business activities.

Jewish textual study and prayer practices reinforce these virtues, as do good religious practices in other religions. Jewish High Holy Days of *Rosh Hashanah* and *Yom Kippur* especially are designed to provide sacred space and time to reflect on how to improve our behaviors.

Mussar is a collection of Jewish spiritual literature that also cultivates inner virtues. One relatively modern *Mussar* teacher, Rabbi Elya Lopian (1876-1970) described *Mussar* as "teaching the heart what the mind already understands.[62]

"Busying" ourselves with *Torah* means to study and live according to the teachings in *Torah*, including also *Talmud*, *Mussar*, and other sacred texts.

Most of us are not familiar with many of these texts. So, of course, we should continually study, and we should consult with our clergy when ethical decisions are unclear.

Good people cultivate good business cultures.

---

[62] MyJewishLearning.org "What is Mussar?"

Do Your Best

> *If you do well, will you not be accepted? And if you do not do well, sin is crouching at the door; its desire is for you, but you must master it.*
>
> - *Genesis* 4:7

You get ahead in business, and life, by doing your best. Doing your best is the essence of how you compete.

Perhaps this sounds obvious, because this virtue is well-known in other contexts including sports. Nevertheless, this wisdom traces back to *Genesis*.

Knowing that we should do our best, however, is one thing. Motivating ourselves to do our best in all situations takes mindfulness. Jewish consciousness of *God* in all matters helps us to maintain such mindfulness.

Doing our best goes hand in hand with competition. Competition is fundamental to free enterprise.

Competition happens when two or more sides are striving for the same thing. Consider, for example, a sales bidding contest. Each side may have somewhat different approaches. They may offer a different set of attributes, positive promises, for their proposed product or service, and they may propose a different price. The sides usually don't know the exact specifications of their competitors' offer.

In open, fair, healthy competition we do our best, and we respect that the best performance wins. We may be cognizant of how our competitor might try to win the customer's order, but our primary focus should be to develop the best customer solution. That should win the customer's order most, if not all, of the time.

What should you say about the other competitor's proposal? Generally, nothing. You should not say negative things about a competitor, especially behind their back.[63]

You can and should highlight positive aspects of your proposal that you believe are true and that you think differentiate yourself from the competition. For example, a contractor may promote how their work teams prepare the jobsite carefully to prevent any damage to existing structure or contents. Or your product is made with totally recyclable materials. Or your service approach is especially user-friendly. Or any number of positive attributes.

But competition that seeks to hurt the other side consciously is malicious. That kind of competition is unhealthy. If you engage in "blood thirsty" competition it ultimately will turn out bad for you.

Torah teaches this through the story of Cain and Abel, the first two sons of Adam and Eve. Abel's business (a shepherd) does well. Cain's business (a farmer) does not do well. Cain, instead of searching his own conscience to seek the root of his failure, blames Abel. Cain seeks to "bury the competition", literally, and he kills his brother. *God* punishes Cain. Cain, no longer a farmer, becomes a wanderer.

In effect, *God*'s "Better Business Bureau" marks Cain as someone with whom you never want to do business.

The Cain and Abel story teaches us, by negative example, what not to do.

We do welcome open competition, and we compete, first and foremost, with ourselves – growing spiritually, increasing our own skills, gaining competence. (The words *competition* and *competent* have the same Latin root.)

"Ambition" is good. Ambition motivates you to do your best. Ambition motivates you to become more competent.

"Greed" is not the same thing. Trying to make money by besting the competition, essentially dividing to conquer, is primitive. Trying to make

---

[63] *Lashon Hara* is Hebrew for "evil tongue". The *Talmud* is very clear that saying bad things about others, even if they are true, is bad behavior. See chapter "*Lashon Hara* (Evil Tongue) Happens".

more and more, to prove worthy if not superior to others, stems from insecurity and misunderstanding.

> Two movies, *"Wall Street"*[64] *and "The Wolf of Wall Street*[65]*"* illustrate how greed corrupts and swallows its protagonists. Both movies are based upon true-to-life stories of men who ultimately went to prison for their financial crimes.
>
> In "Wall Street" the character, Gordon Gekko, says "Greed is Good". Not true. Ivan Boesky, on whom the story is based according to the film's director, was fined $100 million and went to prison for his misdeeds.

Sometimes art is intended to teach us what not to do. Both movies warn about excessive competition, financial maneuvering, and concentration of wealth.

We are required to offer our personal best! When we do our best we receive the appropriate reward – "spiritual capital".

Spiritual capital leads to happiness and may also lead to monetary rewards. But the opposite is not true. Money, by itself, does not ensure happiness.

Spiritually there is a level playing field, and this is founded on the Jewish principle that every person has a direct connection to *God.* (A rabbi's role is not to be our intermediary to *God*, but rather to teach and help us to enhance our own connections with *God.*)

Picture two Jews competing in a business situation. Each of them is doing their best, and each of them believes that they are offering the best alternative. This is healthy competition. Jews have learned from experience, the art of negotiation. We often laugh at ourselves for our intense *hondling,* as we call it in *Yiddish*.

Good negotiation is mutually energizing. It is synergistic. Each competitor takes care of his/her own needs, but there is consciousness

---

[64] "Wall Street", 1987, directed and co-written by Oliver Stone

[65] "The Wolf of Wall Street", Martin Scorcese, 2013

and caring about the needs of the other.

Healthy competition is based upon doing our best and respecting that the other businessperson also is doing their best. Healthy competition leads to better business for both sides. Unlike Cain and Abel, each can help their brother *do well.*

Admit Your Mistakes

Everyone makes mistakes. Mistakes happen, even when we are doing our best. Judaism teaches us to admit our mistakes, apologize to anyone we've harmed, and commit to improving. This is central to Jewish prayer. The *Amidah* (standing) prayer is recited at every Jewish service and includes the following verse.

> *Pardon us, our Father, for we have sinned; forgive us, our King, for we have transgressed; for You are a good and forgiving G-d. Blessed are You Lord, gracious One who pardons abundantly.*
>
> \- *Amidah*[66] verse

A very similar verse would be familiar to Catholics and Protestants from their liturgy.

Yom Kippur (Day of Atonement) is an annual holy day defined in *Torah* which focuses on repentance.

> *On this day shall atonement be made for you, to cleanse you from all your sins; you shall be clean before the Lord.*
>
> \- *Leviticus* 16:30

Before *Yom Kippur*, particularly, Jews are taught to apologize to anyone we may have harmed, even if unintentionally.

This knowledge is particularly important for business leaders. Just as mistakes happen, every business doesn't live up to the expectations of every customer every time. This is inevitable. All we can do as business leaders is to continue improving to meet customers' expectations.

---

[66] *Amidah* is a core Jewish prayer that is said at every service.

When a customer offers a complaint first take that as an opportunity to atone for your business' "mistake". It doesn't matter if your business' failure to meet your customer's expectations was unintentional. Of course, your business meant well. But your customer was dissatisfied. Try to make that right. And try to understand the causes of that customer's missed expectation to make your business better.

Words Matter

God said to Moses, "I am who I am. [67]

- *Exodus* 3:14

According to *Torah*, Moses observed the burning bush, a bush that seemed to be on fire but did not get consumed by the fire. Moses realized this was a miracle, and he asked *God*, "How should I refer to you?" *God*'s reply was the famous verse quoted above.

In Judaism a name is not as simple as how we refer to someone. A name reflects that person's very self.

> *There are three crowns: the crown of Torah, the crown of priesthood, and the crown of royalty, but the crown of a good name supersedes them all.*
>
> - *Talmud* (*Avot* 4:13)

Keter Shem Tov is Hebrew for "The Crown of the Good Name", and it was the title of the first published works of Rabbi Israel Baal Shem Tov's teachings in 1794, the founder of *Chasidism.*

Doing good enhances your reputation, and of course not doing good damages your reputation.

> *From success to failure is one step; from failure to success is a long road.*
>
> - *Yiddish* proverb

This *Yiddish* proverb is very insightful. Reputations can get damaged very easily, and repairing a damaged reputation is arduous and takes a

[67] Some translations are "I am that I am", but the Hebrew actually is future tense. God teaches Moses to be concerned for the future.

long time. Astute businesses build and reinforce their reputation continuously and they put high intrinsic value on their reputation.

Image is important. People, including of course customers and potential customers, are strongly influenced by first impressions. You obviously want to promote an image for yourself and your business which is favorable.

Businesses make up names for their products or brands. The same goes for logos, symbols that stand for the business. Notice that a lot of business advertising is intended to enhance or reinforce the business' image, rather than talking about their products *per se*. A customer may not need a particular product right now, but if they have a positive view of your business then when the time comes to purchase a product the customer will be predisposed to consider your product offering.

It's fascinating that we tend to root for the home-team, in effect the uniforms and colors which are the symbols of the hometown team. When a player leaves to play for a competitor and wears the competitor's uniform they immediately are associated with the competition. Symbols are powerful and enduring.

Business brands are enduring and when well-positioned are very valuable assets.

Religious brands also are enduring. Judaism's symbols such as the *Star of David*, *Menorah* and *Mezuzah* announce to the world, "I am proud of my Judaism". Christianity's *Cross* is similarly powerful.

Everyone will recognize this symbol. It is not pictured in Torah, but from movies and other media we immediately recognize its religious significance and importance.

Reputation similarly plays a big part in how we perceive other people and various businesses.

So, words matter. Words shape how we think about things, about ideas, and about people.

Words also can be limiting. Our very observations about the world are very dependent upon our language, how we describe things.

We tend to treat people who are not proficient in our native language differently, as if they are lacking. The opposite is also true; when we visit a foreign country, we really don't appreciate that foreign culture fully without understanding the local language.

We tend to underestimate people who stutter or who are hard of hearing, as if their difficulty in understanding or speaking our language implies that they lack intelligence.

Businesses miss significant opportunities by not appreciating local language nuances. People in other countries, other than the U.S., usually are more fluent in English than Americans are in "foreign" languages. As a result, many American businesses are at a disadvantage as compared to European and Asian businesses marketing their products in the U.S.

Try not to fall into the trap that your own language is the only language, or the best language. Words become labels. Your imagination and understanding may become prejudiced by labels.

Artists have explored how we can view things when we essentially break the confines of historical frames of reference. Picasso, for example, painted images that intentionally were not representational. In essence, he created a new language for painting. By breaking the bounds of traditional painting vocabulary, he created new kinds of images that pictured what he viewed as the essence of things.

Mathematics is a type of language that communicates ideas (to those that "speak" mathematics). Scientific ideas are often expressed in mathematical terms, largely because underlying assumptions and logical derivation of results can be made clearer using mathematics.

A rabbi once told me, "Praying in Hebrew helps us to feel the prayer". American Jews have a dilemma; Jewish prayers are traditionally chanted in Hebrew, and yet most American Jews do not understand Hebrew. As a result, progressive Jewish religious practices mix English and Hebrew, which possibly misses some of the richness in these traditions. (Catholic prayer services, throughout history, has undergone similar experiences regarding Latin versus local language for prayer services.[68])

"*God*" is difficult to define. That shouldn't be surprising to Jewish thinkers, because Judaism holds *Adonai Echad*, literally "one *God*", to be beyond our full comprehension. In *Torah*, as our opening quote to this section implies, *God* didn't give his name to Moses. This also is why Judaism forbids idols[69]. God is infinite. Any words, painting, or sculpture that attempts to depict God is inherently too limiting.

Orthodox Jews frequently say, "*Baruch Hashem*", meaning Bless the Name. They refer to the name of *God* without saying *God*'s name out of respect.

So, words matter. Names are important. Pictures have impact. All of these are part of your business' image.

Be a Good Loser

"When Bad Things Happen to Good People"

- Rabbi Harold Kushner

Rabbi Kushner's book[70] is often seen at the home of a Jewish family who is sitting *Shiva*[71], the days of mourning after a Jewish burial. How could such a good person die at a young age?

It's beyond our scope, here, to discuss how to console a grieving family member. And we don't want to be cruel by comparing the loss of a loved one to a business deal going badly.

But it's directly on point to consider how you should act when something bad happens. We cannot go back in time, and so we cannot change an

---

[68] Catholic use of vernacular language in liturgical practice after 1964 created controversy. (Wikipedia/Sacred language)

[69] "Do not turn to idols or make for yourselves molten gods; I the Lord am your God." (Leviticus 19:4)

[70] Harold Kushner, When Bad Things Happen to Good People, Avon, January 1, 1983

[71] *Shiva* means "seven". In Jewish tradition at the end of the *Shiva* mourning period (7 days), there is a subsequent period that lasts for 30 days after a death in the family, followed by a one-year period from the death. With each phase the degree of isolation is lessened with the expectation that the mourner will gradually be able to resume normal activities.

unfortunate event after the fact.

What comes next, though, is within our control? How we react to diversity influences our future.

Some business situations that don't go your way seem personal. For example, you didn't get the promotion or the raise that you expected. Or your business team made a great effort to win a sale, but it went to a competitor. Other business losses may seem more indirect, such as world oil prices jumped that suddenly impacted your business' profitability, or a natural weather catastrophe interrupted your supply chain.

Sometimes outcomes are not what we expect and are unexplainable from our point of view. We call that randomness.

> *Random outcomes are manifestations of God's creativity.*
>
> - Rabbi Michael Shevack

We observe randomness in everything.

So, expecting everything to go your way is foolish. When things don't go your way, Jews praise *God*. (Jews take many opportunities to praise God.) Then, we keep going.

> *Pick yourself up, dust yourself off. Start all over again.*
>
> - Jerome Kern[72], 1936

It's not easy to praise *God* when you are depressed just after a business, or other, setback. But we remind ourselves that our mission in life is to make the world a better place, *Tikkun Olam,* literally "repair the world". The world would be boring; indeed, it would not make sense if failures never occurred. We would not have a mission in life.

We recognize this fundamental truth, and therefore we thank *God* for the universe as it is. The gift that it is.

Jews do vary in how they praise *God*:

---

[72] Jerome Kern (1885-1945), a Jewish Broadway composer, composed over 700 popular songs.

> Some Jews ascribe their failing to having sinned in some way. They want to be more worthy of *God*'s favor, and so they try harder.

> Other Jews don't pray so explicitly. They may be uncomfortable personifying *God*, or even uncomfortable praying directly to *God*. They may be introspective enough, though, at a time of loss to examine their own deficiencies.

But the Jewish way is to try to do better. Failures occur, and we should learn from these occurrences. We trust that there will be other opportunities, and we endeavor to do better in the future[73].

Jewish rituals that specifically praise *God* at a time of great loss are a way to work through our tendency to be depressed when a loss occurs. We simultaneously mourn our loss while understanding that such losses are a part of life.

> Upon hearing of a death Jews say, *"Baruch Dayan Ha Emmet"* which in English means "Blessed is the Righteous or True Judge".

At the end of letting ourselves experience sorrow after a death Jews re-enter the world as it is and try again.

Learn from mistakes. Be alert for new opportunities. Try harder next time.

Reflect, Improve, Continue

> *God blessed the seventh day and hallowed it, because on it God rested from all his work which he had done in creation.*
>
> \- *Genesis* 2:3

Sabbath is a pause, a time to reflect. It is not an ending, since the work week starts all over again at Sabbath's end. Besides resting and praying, the weekend is an opportune time for you to reflect on what has gone well at work and what you can make better during the coming week.

---

[73] Other religions also teach similarly.

Besides Sabbath, set aside specific times to assess progress of your business. The context for these periodic business reviews is your business plan.

Many companies prepare annual business plans. They also make a big deal about announcing the plan to the whole employee group. But, too often, the plan goes into a drawer, and day-to-day business crowds out sufficient attention to the goals and necessary key action steps outlined in the business plan.

Make sure your business plan doesn't sit in a drawer. Make sure you review your progress and adjust your activities to meet your goals.

Most companies find it useful to do check their progress monthly or quarterly. For example, monthly you could review your financial results and spot any area where the results are deviating significantly from what you budgeted. On a quarterly basis you could delve more deeply into the progress on key projects. Annually, you would involve the entire organization in the review of progress against planned objectives and update your plan for the coming year accordingly.

The time frame that is practical for introspection and reevaluation depends upon the size of the enterprise. For yourself, utilize each Sabbath for your own introspection. For a business unit a monthly get-together for planning might be practical. And, for a larger multi-unit enterprise a quarterly progress check-up likely would be practical and useful.

> *God* created Earth so that it takes one year to navigate around the Sun, and our seasons are the result of that navigation.
>
> Jewish practices, too, are seasonal. *Shabbat*, sabbath, occurs weekly. The Jewish High Holiday Days, *Rosh Hashanah* and *Yom Kippur*, occur in the Fall. At these sacred holidays in particular, and also in daily prayer services, Jews are taught to reflect upon our past actions, make amends for wrongs that we have done, and recommit ourselves to do better.

New Year's resolutions, occurring each year on a date appropriate for your business, should be sacred for your business. Take this seriously and stick to it.

God is in the Details

> *Her ways are ways of pleasantness, and all her paths are peace. She is a tree of life to those who lay hold of her; those who hold her fast are called happy.*
>
> *- Proverbs 3:17-18*

Torah is complex. It can be read superficially, but it is worth reading carefully. Jews study *Torah*, reread *Torah*, and debate *Torah*. The quality and care in such detailed study makes *Torah* more and more meaningful.

Quality, too, is in the details. Of course, improving business quality is not on a par with studying *Torah,* and we don't mean to equate them.

The lesson here is that quality is more important than a lot of business managers realize. Quality is subtle. Quality is in the eye of the beholder. Improving quality requires study, continual improvement, and attention to details.

For example, most businesses fret over cost comparisons. How does their price compare to their competitor's price? Indeed, price is important. When customers are asked "Is cost an important consideration?" They will say, "Of course". And, when customers are asked to rank considerations about a product they list cost near the top.

Customers do give a lot of weight to cost, perhaps because cost is numerical and easily compared.

But sales don't always go to the lowest bidder.

Customers notice the little details, even if only subconsciously. In fact, quality almost always influences a sale, often very much so.

You may be in an industry in which competition tends to focus on cost. Commodity businesses, for example, presume that cost is the biggest driver, if not the only driver, of sales. Oil, for example, trades on global markets and oil coming from the ground is pretty much indistinguishable from other oil.

But even if you are in such an industry don't fall for this fallacy, or at least take the notion that commodities are indistinguishable from one producer to the next with a grain of salt. There are always quality factors that influence a sale. In the case of oil there are political considerations as well as economic and societal trends that impact the demand for oil. For example, economic expansion generally coincides with increasing oil demand. On the other hand, societal trends to develop and utilize more efficient machinery, including EV automobiles, tends to limit the increase in demand for oil.

Farming, mining and other commodity type industries also each have their own dynamics. So, cost is important, but not the only factor that influences supply and demand.

Customers notice ambiance, style, colors, odors, temperature, and convenience - everything. Customers will point out a detail that doesn't meet their expectation, and they may complain about it. You've no doubt heard the colloquial expression "The devil is in the details". That is an unfortunate colloquialism. A positive saying would be "Fretting the details leads to happy customers".

Nobody likes to hear complaints, but when you do get a complaint listen and learn. "Quality" is all about developing details that add to customers' satisfaction. Quality takes attention and caring.

Quality is all the good things that your business does for your customer, all the product benefits, and all details that go into making your customer comfortable, safe, and ultimately satisfied and happy. When you make your product good and when you improve your customers' experience dealing with you, you are building quality.

Your customer notices quality, even if they don't express it openly. Satisfied customers show appreciation by buying your product, being repeat customers, and hopefully also telling their friends and family about the quality they have experienced.

All the little details count, and little details can add up to a significant competitive advantage. The little details make your reputation.

> *Zabar's*, located on the Upper West Side of Manhattan, has a reputation for excellent white fish salad and other smoked fish delicacies. Customers who live on the Upper East Side even walk

across Central Park to get to *Zabar's*, which is not especially convenient for them. *Zabar's* doesn't advertise cheap deals, and indeed their products are not inexpensive. Besides good food Zabar's value is enhanced by their variety, convenience (at least to Upper West siders), cleanliness, and knowledgeable and friendly staff. *Zabar's* management wisely augments their staffing before Jewish holidays in anticipation of a surge in demand. And, in fact, their excellent reputation builds on itself. Excellence breeds excellence.

Competition, as we have discussed, is both about the business' basic promise and the details that affect the customers interaction with the business.

When the basic promise fails, sales drop off immediately, and it's easy to identify the reason. The product just doesn't work as advertised.

If the details are not just right business sales will fall-off, although perhaps slowly. But customers will notice, and they will remember. Getting back a reputation for good quality will be difficult and take longer.

Not all customers perceive quality the same way. Almost all businesses have customer segments, that is, sub-groups of customers who tend to value particular characteristics similarly and somewhat uniquely as compared to other customers. Often customer segments fall into demographic groupings, such as age, gender, or ethnicity.

Often, economics define segments. Some customers value luxury and are willing to pay for it. Luxury is a matter of degree, though. All customers expect quality.

How you recognize and cater to various customer segments distinguishes your business. Don't expect to cater to all segments. Proactively select and fine-tune your product to target one or two segments.

This is the genius of product marketing. How do you make your targeted customers feel special? And how do you expand your potential marketplace to please more types of customers?

Customer segmentation can lead you to product extensions or perhaps separate branding. Check out *Goldman Sachs'* product offerings[74]. *Goldman Sachs* already has a reputation for catering to institutions and wealthy investors. Drill down on their product offerings, and it becomes apparent how *Goldman Sachs* also is targeting younger families and employees of larger companies. Or check out *Levi Strauss*[75], and see how the "Levi" brand has expanded beyond jeans to additional types and brands of casual clothing.

There is no end to how you can improve your product, no matter which industry you are in. Goodness is in the details. Sweat the details!

God Is Watching

> *Honor your father and mother, that your days may be long in the land which the Lord your God gives you. You shall not kill. You shall not commit adultery. You shall not steal. You shall not bear false witness against your neighbor. You shall not covet your neighbor's house; you shall not covet your neighbor's wife, or his manservant, or his maidservant, or his ox, or his ass, or anything that is your neighbor's.*
>
> \- *Exodus* 20:12-17

Your reputation is precious. How you are perceived impacts not only your business but reflects on your family. What you do and how you do it teaches your children.

Tikkun Olam, the Jewish value of making the world a better place, results from everything that you do. Like your reputation, *Tikkun Olam* builds up over time. Good deeds stack on top of other good deeds.

The opposite is also true. You'll recognize the above quote from the Ten Commandments. Pretty clear laws for what to do and what not to do. Doing one bad thing, especially consciously, can destroy a lot of value.

Never cheat! Honesty is always required. Cheating in business is not

---

[74] Goldmansachs.com/what-we-do/products-and-services

[75] Levistrauss.com/who-we-are/brands

Jewish, at all!

Build trust by doing good. Be proud of everything that you do. Always mean well and be honest and contrite when you make mistakes. Everyone makes mistakes. Learn from your successes and your failures. Continually improve.

Keep the target in mind - do Good. When in a quandary, ask yourself "What would *God* want me to do?"

Put It To Work

Asah (Do)

- Always do your best.
- Never consciously do anything that you know is bad.
- Make it clear to your employees that acting ethically is required, always.
- Decide one thing, or more, that you will do today that will add to the good in your business and in your world.
- Respect your competitor, who presumably also is doing their best
- Compete by being competent. Keep improving.
- Be careful in your choice of words. Words have lasting impact that influence how people view you and your business.

Bara (Create)

- Negotiate fairly, honestly, but earnestly. Go for win-win. Negotiations, done right, should better both businesses.
- When you lose a negotiation, remember this: How does it inform you to make your business, and yourself, better?
- Each weekend review what went well and what did not go so well.

Contemplate what you can do in the coming week to make things better. In this way, try to let the hassles rest, too.

- Determine appropriate times to do a re-evaluation of your business goals, strategy, and progress. Stick to your schedule. Include your managers and employees in these reviews.

- Be sensitive to people who speak other languages, particularly if you intend to sell internationally. How we perceive the world is influenced by our language.

- Price your products/ services competitively, but don't make the mistake of thinking that you must be the cheapest competitor.

- Keep refining the quality aspects of your products/ services. You can always make improvements.

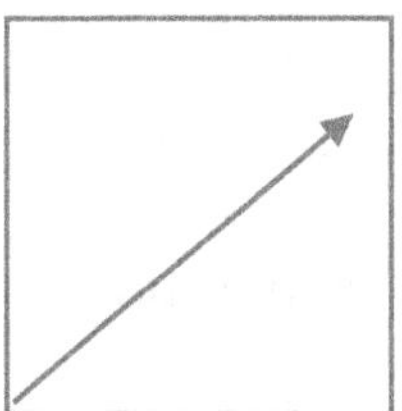

Get a *Minyan*

> *Moses chose able men out of all Israel and made them heads over the people, rulers of thousands, of hundreds, of fifties, and of tens.*
>
> \- *Exodus* 18:25

Moses was taking his father-in-law's advice to delegate responsibilities.

> *Moses' father-in-law said to him, "What you are doing is not good. You and the people will wear yourselves out, for the thing is too heavy for you; you are not able to perform it alone."*
>
> \- *Exodus* 18:17-18

Minyan is Hebrew for "count". Some Jewish prayers services require a minimum of ten adults. The origin of this religious practice is *Genesis* 18:32 in which *God* promised not to destroy *Sodom* if Abraham could find ten innocent men in that city.

Getting a *minyan* for your business is spiritual. Developing a small group of leaders in your business, your business' *minyan*, mirrors Abraham's goal of finding at least ten "innocent" adults. In your business context "innocent" means good people motivated to work together to do good work. "Innocent" implies willingness to learn.

To win in business you must build a team. You cannot do it all by yourself.

In a *minyan* everyone is counted equally. Leading requires listening, delegating, and trusting your team.

Be a Leader

> *One day, when Moses had grown up, he went out to his people and looked on their burdens; and he saw an Egyptian beating a Hebrew, one of his people. He looked this way and that, and seeing no one he killed the Egyptian and hid him in the sand.*
>
> \- *Exodus* 2:11

Rabbi Jonathan Sacks[76], a well-known author and teacher, wrote that leadership according to Jewish principles and values has seven characteristics. With praise and honor to Rabbi Sacks, we paraphrase some of his teachings about Leadership here.

<u>Leadership begins with taking responsibility</u>. Moses saw evil being done, and on his own acted to stop that evil.

A business leader sees opportunities and problems. He or she acts; takes responsibility to seize that opportunity or fix that problem.

<u>No one can lead alone</u>. During the years of wandering in the desert the Hebrews had three key leaders: Moses, Aaron, and Miriam. Moses also got advice from Jethro, his father-in-law.

In business it takes a team to accomplish large goals.

<u>Leadership is about the future.</u> It is vision driven. Moses experienced a vision at the burning bush. He envisioned his role as leading his people out of Egypt and slavery.

Business progress happens when a leader envisions new products or new services and makes it his or her role to achieve that vision.

<u>Leaders learn</u>. Leaders read more and work harder. They set an example.

Business leaders look to other business leaders for good examples. They seek outside advice. They encourage their teammates to work hard by working very hard themselves.

<u>Leadership requires believing in the people you lead</u>. There is a

---

[76] Jonathan Sacks (1948 - 2020) was the chief rabbi of the Orthodox synagogues in the U.K.

difference between power and influence. Power forces people to do things, and it is transitory. You can push people only so long. Eventually people resist being pushed.

Influence requires believing in your teammates. You seek to encourage them to outperform what they would otherwise do by themselves.

Leadership involves a sense of timing and pace.

> *Moses said to the Lord, "Let the Lord, the God of the spirits of all flesh, appoint a man over the congregation who shall go out before them and come in before them, who shall lead them out and bring them in, that the congregation of the Lord may not be as sheep which have no shepherd."*
>
> \- *Numbers* 27:15:17

A leader must lead from the front.

Also, as a leader you need to sense when and how fast your people can progress. People can achieve more than they might think but go too fast and you may lose and exasperate people.

Leadership is stressful and emotionally demanding. There are always setbacks. Some of your people may not stay with you. And things change. New challenges emerge.

In business you are required to be both a leader and a follower. Often at the same time. The whole business is a team. Each department is a team. Each project has a team. Each person within the business succeeds more or less depending upon how they add value to their team(s).

Share the Goal

Developing a staff that is as passionate about your business as you is difficult. It takes patience, training, and leadership. And it requires good communications.

Deuteronomy, the fifth book of *Torah*, is Moses' parting advice to the Hebrews. Moses reminds the Hebrews of *God*'s actions in the past and gives them directions, warnings, and blessings for the future.

Torah tells us that Moses' speech to the Hebrews takes place on the first day of the eleventh month. Business CEO's quite commonly address their team in November or December to recap for them the accomplishments for the past year and getting them motivated to achieve the plan for the upcoming year.

Recaps are effective. So, too, are introductory summary remarks. Effective business speeches, we are taught, start by telling the audience what you are going to tell them, proceed to clearly make the key points, and end by summarizing for the audience what you told them.

Recapping key points is not only for emphasis. Communication studies show that repetition is effective.

Also, various people learn differently. Key messages should be delivered using varying styles and mediums, e.g. written, oral, graphically, etc.

As a business leader spend the time and effort to carefully communicate to your teammates. In this sense, your teammates are like customers. They want to believe in the merits of your business. They want to know how to succeed and make the business better.

Sharing your goals is mutually rewarding. It forces you to be clear, yourself, about the goals you have for the business, and it helps align the motivations of your teammates towards achieving those same goals.

Prepare Future Leaders

> *These were the names of the men whom Moses sent to spy out the land. And Moses called Hoshe'a, the son of Nun, Joshua.*
>
> \- *Numbers* 13:16

Joshua became Moses' successor. Moses selected one man from each of the ancestral tribes to scout the land of Canaan, and each of those men were leaders of their people. But Joshua was special.

Moses had the insight to realize that he needed a successor. *God* directed him to Joshua. From that point onward Joshua was groomed to take over from Moses[77].

Every leader should prepare their successor. In your business (whether you lead a company, division, department, or process) ask yourself three

[77] *Joshua* (1:1–3).

key questions:

Who would succeed you when you leave the business?

Who takes care of the business when you are temporarily unavailable?

Do your people understand and believe in the mission and objectives that you have set for your business function so that whoever takes charge after you can more easily maintain continuity?

Unfortunately, many business leaders fail to prepare adequately for succession. Sometimes it's a matter of not wanting to disappoint other managers who might consider themselves potential successors, or the leader might consciously want a few next-level managers to compete for the promotion to the next higher level.

Many Jewish family businesses have survived and prospered over several generations. Obviously not every family business perpetuates itself successfully, but two beneficial attributes have helped Jewish family businesses prosper multi-generationally. One benefit is that company leadership succession often is clearer. Another more subtle benefit is that strong Jewish values have been cultivated in the family, and as we've discussed throughout this book strong Jewish values are good for personal development as well as business success.

> *I tell you the about the values of my Jewish family business, not simply because I am proud of them. But because I believe that business cannot inject value into society without being driven by a core set of values as well.*
>
> \- Richard Edelman, CEO[78]

Succession planning is not only about identifying who would be the next boss. It also should focus on sustaining the values upon which the business was built by the previous generation.

---

[78] Richard Edleman is CEO of a global communications business that bears his name. His father started the business in 1952. His sister and brother also work at the company

Keep Your Partnerships Clean

> *Two are better than one, because they have a good reward for their toil.*
>
> - *Ecclesiastes* 4:9

Marriage is central to Judaism. Adam and Eve exemplified how man and woman come together to create life. Abraham and Sarah exemplified how man and woman work together to build a family and pass along wisdom and heritage to their children.

Here our purpose is to learn how to do business better. So, why do we talk about marriage? Marriage was the original business partnership, and what is useful and true about getting along in a marriage also is very relevant for your business.

Like a marriage, people have varying roles to play in a business.

In biblical times, the man's and woman's roles were clearer. A woman's day was much devoted to child-rearing, because families were larger and child rearing technologies (all kinds of baby paraphernalia) that save labor had not yet been invented. In contrast, men's time was heavily focused on hunting and tasks which required more physical strength than with today's tools.

Not surprisingly, throughout Jewish history a strong marriage was the best-practice.

> *Shalom bayeet* (Translation: "Peace in the home")
>
> - *Talmud*

"Peace in the home" helps enable familial economic success. This economic modality was reinforced by spiritual thinking, which literally became etched-in-stone in the *Ten Commandments*.

> *Thou shalt not commit adultery.*
>
> - *Exodus* 20:14

Talmud goes into quite a bit of detail about the roles of men and women in a marriage. And, this wisdom, at least by metaphor, applies well to business.

Unfortunately, many Jews are not aware or dismiss *Talmudic* teachings about marriage as outdated, too quaint, or too patronizing. And many *Torah* discussion groups avoid discussing the sexual imagery and symbolism in some of the *Torah* stories, particularly in co-ed discussion groups.

Modern Jewry has the challenge of adapting traditional wisdom to modern societal situations. We can be inspired by tradition, without being bound by it. In this book, we recognize two truisms.

> Women have, and should have, freedom to fully pursue opportunities as they see them. Judaism encourages every person to "talk" to *God* directly and to exercise their Free Will to do good. This applies to family situations as well as to business.
>
> Men and women are different, obviously biologically but also psychologically. Masculine and feminine personality traits are tendencies, although notably with much overlap and variation between the sexes.

At its core, Judaism views "marriage" as a devoted, cooperative, physical model for a familial partnership.

Just as in a marriage, in business we must treat every teammate with honesty, respect, and commitment.

> "Honesty" requires openness to discuss feelings and desires with business partners.
>
> "Respect" requires accepting that each business partner may have varying goals.
>
> "Commitment" requires not breaking promises and dealing with changing circumstances fairly.

Humorously, but deeply meaningfully, the expression *getting in bed with someone* is used to describe an impending business partnership.

A bad business partnership means you are getting "screwed" or, forgive the profanity, "f—d". Power, lust and greed overpower love, care and commitment.

Many businesspeople experience that just at the point of their greatest "success" from having climbed the corporate ladder, there is a serious un-alignment in their personal relationships. Relationship problems may manifest at work or at home, or both. These problems occur when money and power get confused with value. When your values get out of whack *God* requires you to "come back down to earth" to connect with your loved ones and to get your business relationships focused on building good in the world. If these problems are handled, the marital or material "business curve" can continue its ascent. If not, the curve turns downward. Careers can plummet; fortunes can be split in un-amicable divorce, with business partners going separate ways.

These same sins are behind many of the forced break-ups and hostile take-overs that occur in business. So-called business leaders who manipulate others to get promotions or seek prestige and money disproportionate to the actual value that they create are disgraceful. Bribery or cheating, sexual and otherwise, is even more disgraceful. Ultimately, these business leaders, and the businesses that they run, stumble and crumble.

A business partnership is like a marriage. Be faithful, honest, and supportive of your business partners.

If a divorce becomes necessary, whether it be in marriage or business, it should be amicably negotiated.

Make Your Distributors Angels

"Angel" in Hebrew is *mel'eke* which translates as "messenger". (When the message is Good, the *mel' eke* represents *God.*)

In many businesses you don't meet with your end-customer. Rather, a distributor is your intermediary. Your distributor is key to your sales process.

Your distributor represents you. They manifest many of the details that you so much want to do well for your customer.

How your distributor interacts with your end-customer should be way more than just a handoff. Developing a relationship and process with your distributor so that they best represent to your end-customer how you want your product to be presented takes careful and continual work.

Distributors also weigh heavily in quality versus cost tradeoffs for your business. Structurally, distributors should enable your business to reach more customers than you could do on your own. In this sense, distributors may help you increase your revenues which would contribute to lower average costs. But distributors are also businesses; they must cover their own costs and make a profit.

Since the 1980's the Internet has vastly reshaped businesses throughout the world. One driving force is the ability to "go direct". The Internet has become your virtual storefront. Besides developing your business' image your web presence can be a powerful distributor. Web sales can be very efficient, eliminating much of the costs inherent in more traditional sales outlets. And you control your web presence. You control the web sales process details.

These dynamics have reshaped the business competitive landscape, and essentially every business is affected. Manufacturers can go direct. New types of distributors have emerged that make great use of the Internet as well as facilitate the final delivery of products, Amazon being the most successful example.

To help make your distributors angels, treat them like partners.

Dialogue with them to understand their sales constraints. Work with your distributors to develop ways that your product is shown to more prospects and to good advantage.

Understand how your distributors business model necessarily adds costs, and work with your distributor to eliminate any costs that between the two of you are duplicated.

Your distributors know very well how the Internet and social media impact modern sales practices. They have their own websites and advertising materials.

The challenge is to add value to your distributors' business, including their web presence and promotional material, in a way that is mutually beneficial.

And your distributor must add value to you and your end-customer.

You have an obligation to make sure this is so. Otherwise, your business is at high risk of being outdone by a competitor who utilizes the Internet to go direct to the end-customer (disintermediation).

Be Accountable to Each Other

> *And the Lord said to Moses, "See, I make you as God to Pharaoh, and Aaron, your brother, shall tell Pharoah to let the people of Israel go out of his land."*
>
> - *Exodus* 7:1-2

Moses knew his limitations. Moses admitted that his speech was impeded. Perhaps he stuttered. In any case, he was self-conscious of his ability to argue with Pharaoh. *Torah* explains that Aaron, Moses' brother, partnered with Moses as his spokesperson.

Everybody has strengths and weaknesses. As a business leader, know your own weaknesses, and find people to partner with you that fill in the weaknesses on your team. When business team members have complementary strengths there can be great synergy.

Think through your reward systems carefully. Individual excellence should be rewarded, but so too should there be team rewards that emphasizes the importance of working together.

Empower Each Other

> *The tzaddik is one with G-d.*
> *We recognize him because within each of us is also a tzaddik who is one with G-d.*
> *Inside each of us is a spark of Moses.*
>
> - *Lubavitcher Rebbe*, 1977

Tzaddik is Hebrew meaning "righteous person", and is a title given to biblical figures and later spiritual masters. So, *tzaddik* is a rarified title. The chief rabbi, "*Rebbe*", of the *Lubavitcher Chassidic* movement implied that everyone has a bit of the tzaddik in him/ her.

It's common for a leader to be reluctant to delegate responsibilities. You are passionate about your vision. Often, as the entrepreneur you trust your own expertise and judgement over others. And you feel ultimately responsible for the end results.

But you know you cannot do it alone. You must trust the people with whom you share responsibilities.

Train your people as much as practical and be clear with them how their role fits into the overall business plan.

Then, delegate and stand back. Give your teammates adequate resources and authority to complete their assignments. Team members will do their best if they feel empowered and trusted.

Appreciate that each person may go about their tasks somewhat differently than you would do yourself. Their result may be somewhat different than you would have done.

Your role as manager is to coordinate the plans and monitor progress. You need to be available to assist, when requested. This takes humility and patience.

Only God is perfect!

In your business and on any project, everything does not always go according to plan. Missteps are to be expected. That is how the team learns.

You may need to take control if and when it becomes clear that the person to whom the job is assigned is failing. But this requires delicate balance. Jump in too early and you take away your teammates' initiative and enthusiasm.

Teach Each Other

We must teach our children how to swim.

- Talmud (Kiddushin 29a)

According to *Talmud*, a parent must teach their children a trade as well as *Torah*. But it also says that we must teach our children how to swim.[79]

Swimming? Why?

Swimming is a metaphor for navigating the rough waters of life. Swimming requires no support. It requires overcoming fear. When a child learns to swim, metaphorically, they can venture into the uncertain, confident that they can make it to the other side. They gain the confidence to do anything, particularly that which doesn't come naturally or is unfamiliar.

Jews are taught that we should not study *Torah* alone.

> *Two who sit and have words of Torah between them, the Divine Presence is between them.*

- *Talmud (Avot* 3:2)

A teacher guides us, and a study partner forces us to communicate what we have learned clearly.

But ultimately the purpose of teaching is to give the pupil the skills and courage to learn for themselves. Teaching gives the pupil tools to keep on learning.

This is so important in modern business, because the pace of growth in knowledge is so rapid. What I learned in college is largely obsolete now, because computerization (and now artificial intelligence) tools are more efficient. This is true for many of us.

Businesses that are very innovative, by design, are pushing the limits of current knowledge. So, we must teach our students, and our workmates, how to learn.

---

[79] Rabbi Dan Moskovitz: Commentary on Genesis 25:19-28. (ReformJudaism.org)

Listen to Each Other

And when Moses heard this, he was content.

- Leviticus 10:20

Aaron was directed by Moses to do something, but Aaron didn't quite follow Moses' directions. Aaron explained his rationale to Moses, and Moses listened. Realizing Aaron's intentions, Moses accepted and agreed with Aaron.

How often do we essentially close our minds even though we are supposedly listening? We may be distracted. We may be so confident in our own thinking that we are not open-minded. As parents we can often tell when our kids are nodding their heads, but not really paying attention to us.

Listening and hearing go together.

If we value the other persons worth, we must make sure that we are listening and hearing.

When we truly listen to the other person we show our regard for them. Then, if we argue back the other person is more likely to listen to us.

We've previously mentioned the *Shema*, a declaration that Jews recite at least twice every day. The *Shema* starts "Hear O' Israel". The *Shema* teaches us a lot, but one lesson is that before you say something important pause for a moment to make sure your audience is listening.

Put It To Work

Asah (Do)

- Put a lot of priority on finding the best teammates available.

- Share your vision and plans with your team. Make sure each team member knows their role.
- Delegate responsibilities and give space and show patience so that your teammates learn to succeed on their own.
- Be kind to yourself. Leadership is stressful. Rest and use Shabbat, sabbath, to recharge yourself.
- Cooperate fully, forthrightly, with your co-managers, employees, and investors. These people constitute your business family.
- Reward your team as a group for team successes.
- Never stop learning and encourage your teammates to continue learning.

Bara (Create)

- Examine your work roles. Acknowledge for yourself those in which you are the leader and those in which you are the follower. Be good at both.
- Try to put together a team in which various people's skills and experience complement each other.
- Your middlemen reflect you. Work backwards by thinking like a customer to review and improve how your customers view both your middlemen and you.
- Coach your employees how to represent your product to the best advantage.
- Dialogue with your distributors to train them about your product and to understand their needs as an intermediary. Also, listen to your distributors to find out how your end customers feel about your products and services.
- Be flexible. If a teammate poses a dissenting viewpoint or approach, make the effort to understand their opinion.

- What would happen to your business if you were not able to work? Make your contingency plan just in case that day comes sooner than you expect.

- Take pride in training and preparing your successor.

- Even if a protégée leaves your company, still be proud of what that person has accomplished. If you can, maintain a relationship with that person(s) who no longer works with your directly.

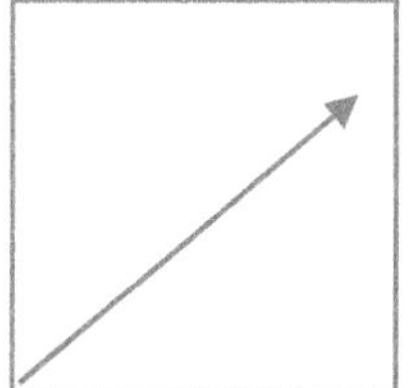

Love Your Customers

When two people relate to each other authentically and humanly, God is the electricity that surges between them.

- Martin Buber[80]

God takes pride in each person. The wise businessperson takes this to heart. Recognize the *God*-like quality in each person and you will feel genuine empathy for them. This is the overarching secret to good marketing.

Most of your customers are strangers to you first. It takes a process to welcome the stranger, engage with them to determine their needs, and satisfy them.

Invite the stranger to become familiar with your offerings.

Engage with them to see if there is a potential match between their needs and your capabilities. Kindly but diligently pursue them as leads if there is a potential fit. Ask them to become a customer.

Satisfy each customer's needs. Fulfill your promises to them. Continue to show your genuine interest by following up with your customers.

Recognize that each customer is somewhat unique. So, no matter how finicky, how demanding, is your customer treat them courteously and helpfully.

[80] Buber was an Austrian-Jewish and Israeli philosopher. He was nominated several times for Nobel prizes. His most famous work was "I and Thou" written in 1923.

Know Your Customers

How your business perceives its customers and their needs defines your business. In turn, how your customers view your business and what it offers defines your business' value.

Consequently, every business should learn as much as practical about its customers to better understand their needs.

Every business also must believe that its products are beneficial to its customers. And the business' products need to be continually improved. What is satisfactory today no doubt will be surpassed in the future by better products and services.

Moreover, your business' obligations to its customers go beyond just satisfying the customer.

> *When you build a new house, you shall make a parapet for your roof, that you may not bring guilt of blood upon your house if anyone fall from it.*
>
> \- *Deuteronomy* 22:8

Your business has obligations to not sell dangerous products. Part of your obligation is to know your customer enough so that you are reasonably sure that the customer is qualified to handle your product.

So, for example, you wouldn't sell firearms or alcoholic beverages to minors. Also, if you sell dangerous products your labeling needs to clearly spell out the dangers, and your packaging must be secure to prevent accidents.

Your obligations as a seller are more subtle but similarly important if you are selling a product that requires special expertise. Notice, for example, that a pharmacist asks if you would like instructions when you buy a prescription drug. Or, if you utilize a financial advisor hopefully your advisor interviewed you to learn your needs, your familiarity with various types of investments, and your attitudes about risk taking. When you buy a new car, the dealer should instruct you about the interior workings of the car's controls.

"Know Your Customers", or "KYC", is a legal requirement in the United States, and similarly imposed in other countries, that financial firms obtain proper identification from each of their customers. The government's intent for these requirements is to to prevent money laundering.

Ethically, businesses have responsibilities that go beyond verifying a customer's identity. A financial business should not sell an investment which is too risky and therefore unsuitable for a particular customer. No business should sell a product to a customer which is so expensive that it is clearly beyond what a customer can afford.

Market Segmentation

> *The art of marketing is largely the art of brand building. When something is not a brand, it will be probably be viewed as a commodity.*
>
> - Phillip Kotler, Jewish Humanist and Marketing Professor

The more you know about your customers the more you will see various customer segments. Obviously, demographics, territory, and price points are potential characteristics that may define a segment. But psychographics and other subtle characteristics also may be important to define segments.

Take, for example, women's clothing. This is a very large market, and one in which there already is a lot of market segmentation. My wife is petite and knows which stores stock petite sizes. Other women, obviously, shop where over-size garments are available. Teenage girls like different styles than young mothers, and both age groups have different preferences than older women. Styles can be bold and modern or conservative and more subdued. Casual clothes are different than clothes more appropriate for the office. Some stores specialize in women's dresses for special occasions, but even here prom dresses are different from wedding dresses, bridesmaid dresses, and mother of the bride dresses. Specialized activities like yoga, skiing, camping tend to require specialized clothing, and there are stores that target these special use clothes. The segmentation possibilities go on.

Note that you cannot sell everything. Department stores tend to carry lots of items but notice that within department stores there are stores within the store. Also, even department stores specialize by price point and other characteristics.

Professor Kotler also advices,

> *No company in its right mind tries to sell to everyone.*

And,

> *All customers are important, but some are more important than others.*

- Philip Kotler

In most businesses a small fraction of customers generates a relatively large portion of sales. So, pay special attention to to those.

The clever merchant captures customers' birthdays and sends them notices for their birthday. They try to know that a particular customer likes cruises, or waits for sales, or shops on the weekends, or other idiosyncrasies. Gather this type of information as much as practical. Utilize it to single out your best customers within your chosen segment and make those customers feel special.

Build your brand to make it easy for prospective customers to anticipate what they will find when they shop at your store.

Ask your best customers to recommend you to their friends or on social media.

Make Technology Your Distributor

> *One secret of success in life is for a man to be ready for his opportunity when it comes.*

- Benjamin Disraeli[81]

---

[81] Disraeli (1804-1881) was twice Prime Minister of the U.K. Disraeli was proud of his Jewish ancestry, although his father had him baptized as a Christian when he was 13, when a Jewish boy normally would become *Bar Mitzvah*. That historical quirk, however, allowed Disraeli to become a member of Parliament, because before 1858 Jews were not permitted to hold public office in the U.K.

As already discussed, the Internet is reshaping distribution in almost every industry. Seize this opportunity in your own business.

On-line selling has advantages of being cheaper and enabling the company to present themselves and their products precisely. It also can seem impersonal, although as on-line selling gets better many companies are able to establish close customer relationships.

> *MTailor* is both a manufacturer and a distributor of men's clothing. They utilize computer technology to enhance both their manufacturing and their selling. Using an app *MTailor* customizes their clothing to fit the individual. And their sales are entirely on-line.

To the extent that your business requires face-to-face sales, you still can leverage technology to make it easier and better for your customers. This might include scheduling appointments, providing for virtual sales calls when that is convenient for your customers, making it easier for your customers to re-order, and confirming orders or following up on complaints.

If you are in a distribution business, it is even more important to adapt and develop technology for your business. Endeavor to become so effective that your manufacturers or product suppliers see the value that your company delivers. Otherwise, your business eventually will be disintermediated, i.e. replaced.

If you are in a service business, there also are opportunities to utilize technology to improve your business processes. Notice that physicians more and more utilize telephone conferences to triage their patients. Engineers and designers utilize more advanced modeling to develop and display their work to their clients. News organizations utilize streaming, webcasts, and specialized newsletters to target and reach their customers.

Market Research

When businesses were smaller the shopkeeper knew his or her customers well. Customers were neighbors. Customers who regularly shopped at a particular store, say a grocery store, ran a tab.

> My mother got a standard order from the local deli which was

delivered to our door each Saturday. No cash changed hands on Saturday, and there was no *Visa* charge. My mother settled her bill once each month directly with the deli. The deli's market research was informal. The deli owner knew our family and was confident that my mother would pay the bill in full each month.

Today, at the other end of the scale, we shop on-line. We try to support our local economy, but invariably we buy many items from *Amazon* or other large chains. These large stores know my buying history. They push advertisements to me about items that they think I will rebuy or an item that I casually researched on-line. This is done automatically backed up by huge databases and sophisticated artificial intelligence.

No matter the size of your business gathering information about your customers is key. Customer data is important to enable your business to:

Identify and refine your market segments.

Be more efficient coordinating with your suppliers or your own manufacturing department.

Be proactive in contacting prospective customers.

Be more efficient during the sales process.

Be more proactive and effective to ensure that your customers are satisfied with your products and services.

Put It To Work

Asah (Do)

- Keep records about each customer and, as practical, each prospect. Keep track of each customer's demographics and purchase history.
- Interact with your customers both before the sale and after.
- Pay attention to social media. React in a positive way to address any complaints that you get on social media and try to utilize the social

media platform to communicate that you are always trying to improve.

Bara (Create)

- Make the Internet part of your distribution system.
- Utilize the telephone effectively. While this is old technology it is familiar to all customers and can be very useful to enhance service. At the same time, recognize that impersonal telephone techniques, such as phone trees, can turn off certain customers.
- Be aware that various age groups will gravitate to texting, email, or voice differently.
- Test significant investment decisions utilizing market research. Get advice on how to conduct market research.

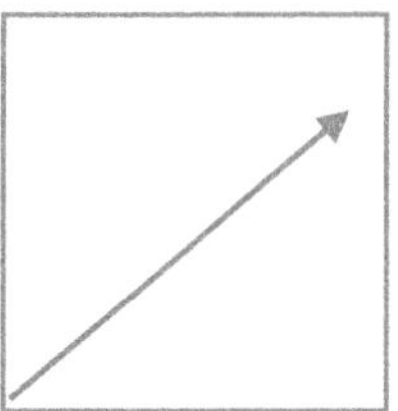

Selling Is Helping

Love your customer as yourself.

- A variation of *Leviticus* 19:18

Marketing texts often list Four "P's" (Product, Pricing, Place, Promotion) to summarize key selling suggestions, and more recently some authors cleverly have added other P's (People and Process).[82]

Hopefully you've learned throughout this book that good business is based upon more than even these "P's". Think of these six "P's" as components of your sales strategy. But go beyond these tactics with an overall sales mission.

Think of sales as a spiritual transaction. Add value to your customer. How do you do that? "Love your customer as yourself", and "Do good"! You are developing a relationship with another person; helping them; and improving their life.

Sales transactions are getting more complicated as parts of the transactions are moving on-line. Still, the basic guidelines and sales mission applies. The computer should be an extension of yourself, so you want to make the computer as *hamish*, friendly, as possible.

Within every business, people and departments interact with each other. Internal departmental transactions are essentially sales transactions, too. So, everyone is a salesperson.

We, all, can be better salespeople. It takes training, practice, and a conscious effort to help your customer.

[82] Alexandra Twin, *Investopedia*, March 2023

Everybody is a Salesperson

Chutzpah (audacity) seasoned with charm translates as enthusiasm.

- *Yiddish* saying

Business is all about sales. And everyone is a salesperson! Every day!

There is no buyer without a seller. There is no seller without a buyer. It takes two sides to make the product worthwhile. It takes two sides to create the manifestation of a product.

In fact, it takes two sides, many times sequentially, for most products to reach the end user. Products usually involve many layers and handoffs from raw material to finished goods. Specialized businesses supply raw materials, and intermediary businesses are involved in distribution and retail. Sales are involved at each step. Food, for example, starts with a farmer (or fisherman or rancher). The farmer buys seed, fertilizer and farm implements from other businesses specializing in selling to the needs of farmers. The farmer sells to an intermediary food processing company, such as a milk processing and packaging business. The food processor in turn sells to a food distributor company, who trucks the food products throughout the country. The food is sold to a retail grocery, and finally the grocery sells the milk to you to take home.

Service businesses are similarly varied and involve layers of suppliers and end providers. For example, physicians buy medical instruments from medical providers. Your doctor "sells" you the service of examining you and diagnosing your illness. You select a pharmacy to which your physician sends a drug prescription for you.

And, within most companies there are many handoffs between co-workers and departments. These are sales, of sorts, too. One person has created something of value, and the other person accepts that product. Each handoff moves the product along its way to the end customer, hopefully adding value as it goes, called the "value chain".

Sales situations also arise in negotiations in which businesspeople engage every day. We don't think of negotiations as "sales", but that is what a negotiation ultimately is. One side, the "seller", has a point of view, and is arguing to another, the "buyer", to get agreement. You may be negotiating with a supplier for an amount of raw material, unit costs, or delivery time. Or you may be arguing a point-of-view related to your business. You may be selling a critical idea that affects the overall business, such as how to interpret recent business results or whether to increase prices. Or you may be selling something less intrinsic to the end-product but nevertheless important, such approval of a budget, a hiring request, a raise, etc.

So, be enthusiastic about selling. Have the confidence to ask your customers about their needs and be open to their critiques. Develop sales relationships.

Sales Training

Confidence is half of victory.

- *Yiddish* saying

A successful salesperson doesn't get dismayed when a potential customer says, "No". That salesperson probes to understand the prospect's sales objection. That becomes a learning experience.

Sales is a process, and every person in business should learn sales techniques. It is worthwhile to take sales training courses, which is beyond our scope here. Nevertheless, the sales process generally has four phases[83]:

Prospecting and Qualification: Identify potential customers and learn enough about them to determine whether you and your product are a good fit for them. You engage with these prospects sufficiently to understand whether they recognize that they have a real need and truly want to learn of a solution to their need.

Presentation and Handling Objections: You formulate what you think matches your prospect's needs. You present your solution to your prospect, and you probe to understand from their point of view whether in fact your product is good for them.

Closing the Deal: You ask for agreement, and you are clear with your

[83] oneflow.com

customer what you will do and what they need to do. This should not only be about price.

Follow-up and Relationship Building: Selling to existing customers is easier than selling to a brand-new prospect. Your past customers know your value and presumably have been satisfied. As you learn more about your customers you should be able to offer them additional products and services.

Each of these steps requires attention and practice. For example, when I was a consultant, I experienced what could be called the "proposal writing trap". A prospect can easily say, "Get me a proposal", but that may just be a way for them to gather information or just to get you to go away.

Sometimes it's worthwhile to give away information to build trust with a prospect. At least once, I was called by a prospect one year later that I had essentially written off. They now had a need and remembered me. I got the call and got the job - one year later. The lesson here is always to be gracious and follow-up with prospects, even when you seemingly lose the sale.

Imagine yourself in the other person's shoes. How would you perceive the sales pitch that you, yourself, are making? What would be your questions, your objections? Ask questions to make sure you understand your buyer's point of view. Listen. Answer your buyer's questions openly, frankly, and truthfully. Be flexible and patient and kind. You won't make every sale but do these things and unquestionable your sales success rate will be better.

Control the conversation. But listen carefully. This is the art of selling.

Pricing is important, though the wise businessperson knows that pricing is only part of good marketing. Sales don't always go to the lowest bidder. When you compete only on price you also eventually lose based upon price.

Selling is all about relationship building, problem solving, and having empathy with your customer.

Sell Fairly

And you shall take no bribe, for a bribe blinds the officials, and subverts the cause of those who are in the right.

- *Exodus* 23:8

You shall not steal, nor deal falsely, nor lie to one another.

- *Leviticus* 19:11

These commandments in *Torah* are clear. You cannot steer a customer to an inferior product nor to a product just because secretly you would earn a higher profit margin. Neither behavior would be consistent with "love your neighbor as yourself" or with the commandments in *Torah* listed above.

Honesty is not only the best policy[84], it is the only acceptable policy. Good Jewish businesspeople compete by developing and selling products and services that are desirable. Higher profit margins are not deserved unless a product or service is better than what others offer.

Transparency is the key. Your customer should not be fooled, at least not intentionally.

An Educated Consumer is our Best Customer

- Sy Syms[85]

Win business and sleep better at night by competing based upon better products and better sales experiences for your customers. That, really, is the Jewish way.

---

[84] "Honesty is the best policy" is sometimes attributed to Benjamin Franklin or Thomas Jefferson, as this maxim was popular in the 17th century. Note, however, that the essence of this maxim clearly is stated in *Torah*.

[85] Syms Corp. was founded by Sy Syms (1926–2009), who was born Seymour Merinsky. Syms Corp. grew substantially throughout the 1980's and 1990's. Sadly, it went bankrupt in 2011, two years after Sy passed away.

Competitors Make You Better

Who is wise? He who learns from every person.

- Ben Zoma, rabbinic sage[86]

Jewish law favors open competition. Considering that much of Jewish law dates back centuries, it is quite remarkable how egalitarian were these laws.

Competition is presumed to lower prices and to ensure a plentiful supply of quality goods, which is good for consumers. Consequently, Jewish law looks skeptically at any business rule that is intended to suppress competition.

Monopolies or any restrictive agreements are disallowed unless there is an over-riding benefit to society. Exceptions are limited, but nevertheless are made for practical reasons when it is recognized that pure open competition causes ethical complications.

The basis for Jewish business law recognizes the fundamental principle which we've discussed throughout this book:

> *God* is the originator and owner of all wealth, and mankind only has stewardship of material goods with *God*'s blessing.

This principle is over-arching. Morality and kindness are always required. Some might say, "*God* is watching."

Jewish law does permit some restrictions on competition for a limited time when necessary to mitigate the destruction of another person's livelihood. For this reason, local businesses are given some preferences over strangers.

> Local residents cannot be restricted from opening a new business, except in unusual circumstances where a town is so small that it cannot support two similar businesses.

---

[86] Simeon ben Zoma was a rabbinic sage of the 1st and 2nd century. This quote is also often attributed to Benjamin Franklin, who was not Jewish but wisely learned from good Jewish sources.

> Strangers may face some additional restrictions to protect the existing local businesses, but a potential competitor cannot be restricted from competing if they offer a superior product.

Today's business environment is much more complicated, and rabbis may differ on how to apply *Talmudic* principles to today's business situations. Each situation would weigh the preference for open competition, while recognizing that local, existing businesses should be protected where practical. In the long-run, practicalities would give way to the expansion of competition that is seen to benefit the whole of society.

For example, *Talmud* recognizes that in large cities where many competitors in a similar business already compete, there is no rationale to exclude one more competitor. Consider, then, that today in many industries direct selling techniques reach remote customers already. In effect there already are a lot of competitors in these industries operating in every community. This trend has been increasing for decades, accelerated by the Internet. The physical location of a business has become much less relevant.

Many towns have zoning, licensing, and signage rules that may be seen as limiting competition. To the extent these types of restrictions have valid safety benefits they would be justified. Some restrictions also may be permitted for esthetic reasons if they are judged to benefit the whole society. For example, some communities impose restrictions on signage sizes, lighting, and even building heights to impose a common, and presumably preferable, esthetic.

Jewish law considers it unfair to the existing local businesses if somehow a new competitor entrant could escape paying local taxes.

> *Citizens cannot restrict entry of others if newcomers are willing to accept their share of taxes.*
>
> \- Maimonides, *Torah* scholar in Middle Ages

Out -of-state sales complicate how local sales taxes are applied, and this can raise fairness issues. Jewish law would not condone a business shipping their goods from out-of-state for the sole purpose of escaping paying local taxes.

Other restrictive sales practices also are considered unfair, and therefore prohibited under Jewish law. For example, it is permissible to entice a potential customer walking past your business, but you cannot enter a competitor's place of business to approach potential customers there.

Bottom line, competition is inevitable! And you should only expect to win in business by competing fairly. Essentially, you win when your products are better.

You also should take it for granted, unless proven otherwise, that your competitor's motivations are similar to yours. They are proud of their business; they are honest; they work hard; and they strive to support their family. Like you, they play a legitimate role in commerce. And they, like you, are morally entitled to profits that are earned fairly.

Learn from them! Make your product better, continually. Understand situations in which your competitor beats you. When you lose an important sale ask yourself what you could have done better? Why was your competitor's product perceived to provide more value to that prospective customer? Could you have communicated better with your prospective customer? How should you modify your product improvement plans going forward?

It's fair game to reverse engineer your competitor's product, as long as you act fairly in doing so. You cannot steal trade secrets. You should not try to pry proprietary information about your competitor from your competitor's employees. But you can purchase your competitor's product, take it apart and otherwise analyze it. If you are in the restaurant business, for example, you can eat at your competitor's restaurant.

Trade associations are common, and you can learn a lot by attending trade shows and other trade association events. Keep in mind though, that collusion and restriction of trade practices in the U.S. are not lawful.

Jews are obligated to obey the Law of the Land. You cannot preplan prices with your competitor nor agree to subdivide your marketing territory so that each of you effectively has a monopoly in that subdivided territory.

In summary, respect your competitor. Learn from them. Beat them in business fairly by improving your own products and services.

Shalom[87] (Hello)

And the Lord appeared to him by the oaks of Mamre, as he sat at the door of his tent in the heat of the day. He lifted up his eyes and looked, and behold, three men stood in front of him. When he saw them, he ran from the tent door to meet them, and bowed himself to the earth, and said, "My lord, if I have found favor in your sight, do not pass by your servant. Let a little water be brought, and wash your feet, and rest yourselves under the tree,
while I fetch a morsel of bread, that you may refresh yourselves, and after that you may pass on--since you have come to your servant." So they said, "Do as you have said."

- *Genesis* 18:1-5

Hospitality, known as *hakhnasat orchim* in Hebrew, is considered one of the most important Jewish values. Perhaps no detail is more important than how your business welcomes each customer, whether they are a new prospect or repeat customer.

First impressions matter. New prospects are wary. They are not sure they are in the right place. They probably are not ready to buy right away. They are checking you out.

Repeat customers are like gold to your business. They obviously like something about your business. Yet, they need reassurance that they've made the right decision. If you welcome a repeat customer by name, you send an immediate signal that you value them.

Remembering people's names is very important in Jewish culture. Remembering someone's name dignifies them. In this vein, Jews traditionally name their children after deceased relatives as a

[87] "*Shalom*" is Hebrew. Translated to English "*shalom*" means "peace" or "hello". In the 1960's the hippies peace sign used in greeting others conveyed both meanings. Similarly, in Israel peace is always top-of-mind.

remembrance and an honor.

Introduce yourself to new clients and ask to know their names. Pay attention to learn their name. Paying attention is like telling your brain to write it down and file their name away for later use.

Say "Hello" with a smile, and, if possible, address your customer by name. Teach this practice to your employees.

> A women's health clinic depended heavily upon government stipends, and the amount of funds from the government to the clinic was based upon the number of patients treated. The manager of the clinic made it a priority that every patient be addressed by name when they entered the clinic, insisting that all the staff follow her lead in doing so. The result was a significant increase in clients. Repeat patients became more likely to return, and there even was an increase in the number of new patients. The quality of the medical staff didn't change. What changed was that patients perceived a more welcoming atmosphere.

Your website and your social media also help form customers' first impressions of your business. If a customer comes to your physical workplace, you can bet that they've already been to your website. Your website is your virtual storefront. Make it welcoming and useful.

Some businesses inherently foster a close relationship between seller and buyer. For example, medical providers have perhaps the most personal relationships with their patients. Financial advisors and clergy similarly are in positions to foster a very close relationship with their customers (clients or congregants). But, even in these most personal types of situations the best providers, (doctors, accountants, or rabbis), do better if they consciously and conscientiously personally remember their customers.

Little details become big influencers when they don't get performed well.

> Years ago, my wife Carol and I moved from Chicago to a suburb in Southern New Jersey. We were looking to join a synagogue, and we attended a nearby synagogue several times. At some point the rabbi approached us after services but acted as if he had never seen us before. Did he not notice us the previous times? We didn't feel especially welcomed. We joined a different synagogue.

Contrast that welcome with the following, also true, personal experience.

> I approached a saleswoman at a car dealership where a few years before we had purchased a new car. The saleswoman greeted me, "Hi, Joel. Good to see you. How is Carol enjoying her car?" The result: Over many years we have purchased three new cars from that dealer, and each time we were sure to deal with that same salesperson.

Even better than remembering customers' names, make it your business to remember something relevant about each customer. Put that into your welcome.

Many people, me included, have difficulty remembering names. Train yourself to remember names better. Where practical utilize software or other tools to collect details about your customers.

> State Farm is the largest insurer in the U.S. Their sales agents are very well trained. They were taught, even before computers were ubiquitous, to maintain index cards for each client with pertinent information on the index card. So, if you were to call them, they would quickly find your index card on their Rolodex to familiarize themself with key details about you. I suspect they still teach their agents how to utilize computerized customer records to personalize their conversation with you.

You might think that businesses with seemingly small, quick transactions would not be able to establish close customer relationships. Not so.

> Starbucks'[88] app is one of the most downloaded restaurant apps, and the app provides a personalized ordering experience.
>
> Starbucks remembers customers 'favorite drinks and preferences and rewards them with perks and freebies based on their preferences and past activity. Starbucks uses an AI algorithm to send personalized messages to their customers.

---

[88] Starbucks has Jewish roots. It was founded by Jerry Baldwin, Gordon Bowker, and Zev Siegl, opening its first store in 1971. Howard Shultz joined Starbucks as head of marketing in 1981, emphasizing personalized selling from his start there. Starbucks went public in 1992 with Shultz as CEO, and the company grew to become the largest coffee house chain in the world.

You will remember names better by consciously repeating a new acquaintance's name when they are introduced. Try to associate their name with something about them. It's a matter of telling your brain that remembering this name is important.

> My father, *alav hashalom*[89], was a wedding photographer. When I was a child and went to a restaurant with my family, invariably my father would excuse himself and go up to seemingly strangers and say, "Pardon me, but I took pictures at your wedding. Was your maiden name "Schwartz" and your husband's name "Cohen"? The people would be amazed and flattered. These people invariably came back to my father's studio to have pictures taken for their child's bar or bat mitzvah, the Jewish coming of age ritual for a child when they reach age thirteen. My father prided himself on the studio delivering a quality photo album, but no doubt his business benefited by sweating the details, including remembering customers' names.

Care about the stranger, and show you care by remembering their name.

Le'hitraot (See You Again)

Just as you make "hello" important and friendly, make your goodbye friendly. *Shalom* actually means both hello and goodbye. *Le'hitraot* is another way of saying goodbye in Hebrew and conveys that you look forward to seeing them again.

Think how impressive it is to a stranger, a new prospect, if you not only say "goodbye" in a friendly way, but you mention their name in your goodbye salute. When you do this, you subtly say, "You are important to me. We just met, and I remember your name."

When a customer makes a large purchase your "goodbye" and "thank you" ratify for that customer that they made a good choice. Do you know who looks the most closely at automobile ads? People who have recently purchased a new car. They aren't looking to buy a new car. They are looking for ratification, perhaps unconsciously, that they made a smart purchase.

> When we were first married, we lived in several apartments. Eventually, we purchased a house. The real estate agent sent us a

---

[89] Hebrew meaning "May peace be upon him/her."

housewarming gift, a vase with flowers. This was a classy "leitraot", and a thoughtful way to tell us that we made a good purchase.

Say goodbye with a smile. When you say "see you later" mean it. "*Le'hitraot*".

Be Proud (and Not Too Humble)

An intelligent mind acquires knowledge, and the ear of the wise seeks knowledge.

- *Proverbs* 18:15

You have a great product. You've worked hard, and you've invested a lot of money to develop your store and build your inventory. Can you, should you, advertise? Of course!

Advertising's purpose is to get a customer's attention. As long as you confidently feel your product will benefit a particular customer you are doing them a favor by capturing their attention. You are helping them. This is a *mitzvah!*

Mitzvah is Hebrew literally meaning "commandment", but *mitzvah* also is utilized to mean "good deed". In Judaism, following *God*'s commandments and doing good deeds are really the same thing.

The *Talmud* discusses many selling situations, including what is permissible and what is not.

You cannot sell what you know to be a bad product. And you cannot sell a product to someone for whom you know your product is not a good fit. That would be stealing. Do not steal!

- *Talmud*

But you can and should proudly advertise your product.

While you are bragging about your product, you cannot denigrate your competitor.

- *Talmud*

If you are truthful and well-meaning, you are on firm ethical ground. With this in mind, let's go through a few examples.

Can you exaggerate, say, by playing loud music or using bright colors to draw attention to your store? Yes. You are not hurting anybody by doing so. In fact, by getting your customers' attention towards your product, which you truly believe is good, you are doing a service.

Can you polish your gems? Can you shine bright lights on your products to make them shine? Yes. But you cannot deceitfully do this. Everyone knows that jewelers have bright lights on their jewelry cases, and that cosmetic counters use bright flattering lights to show their make-up to best advantage. Car dealers shine their showroom cars. But you cannot do this deceitfully.

> *You shall not curse the deaf or put a stumbling block before the blind.*
>
> - *Leviticus* 19:14

You cannot cover up a blemish on your product, or otherwise hide a known defect. If your product is used, you must disclose this fact.

Can you use sex appeal to sell your product? Yes. This is a form of grabbing attention. But you cannot take advantage of the model in your ad, and you cannot be crude or abusive or offensive.

Can you charge a higher price than your competitor? Yes. You can charge a fair price reflecting your costs of doing business. We'll talk about fair pricing in a later section.

Can you put items on sale? And can you discount some items to bring people into your store and catch their attention for another product that is not on sale. Yes. This is another form of grabbing attention, and it is ethical as long as it is not deceitful. Everyone knows that sale items may be placed next to the newest and greatest model that is not on sale. But remember, you cannot lie. You cannot say that your price is the lowest in town, if that is untrue.

Can you hand-out samples? Yes. This is a form of a sale. But obviously, you cannot hand out addictive products, like a habit-forming drug.

You must be especially scrupulous regarding children. You should not give a child something, like candy, that might be harmful to them or without their parents' permission.

Sales contests and promotions also can be worthwhile, good practices, but only if they are fair and scrupulous.

Ask yourself, "Would my customer buy this item if they knew something about the product that I know and am not telling them?" It's always best to fully inform your customer. Caveat emptor (buyer beware) is not valid, or certainly is limited, according to Jewish law.

Put It To Work

Asah (Do)

- Never be dishonest.
- Recognize that every interaction with other people is a selling situation.
- Learn selling techniques.
- Work on your presentation techniques. First impressions matter.
- Say hello with a smile to everyone entering your business.
- Train your employees that they have a sales role and teach them these steps.

Bara (Create)

- Whenever practical, ask your customers why they like the product they have just bought from you. And, when you lose a sale try to ask why.
- Don't shift blame to your employees when a sale is lost. Sales is a team effort. Share mutual successes and utilize failures as learning experiences.
- Be especially alert to trends in your business, changing tastes or customer needs..
- Practice remembering people's name. Turn the perfunctory meeting ritual into an opportunity to learn something about a stranger.
- Find and utilize a practical record keeping tool that you can access on your phone and computer to readily retrieve pertinent information

about people you meet.

- Maintain a relationship with past customers. Send them News Year's cards, and if practical birthday best wishes.
- Ask customers if they are pleased with their purchase and ask them to help you get even better by telling you what they liked a lot and not so much.
- Seek to make every interaction a win-win negotiation.
- Test with customers and prospective customers, including with people who choose not to buy from you, how you and your product were perceived.
- Try to put yourself in a potential customers position to judge how you and your product may be coming across.

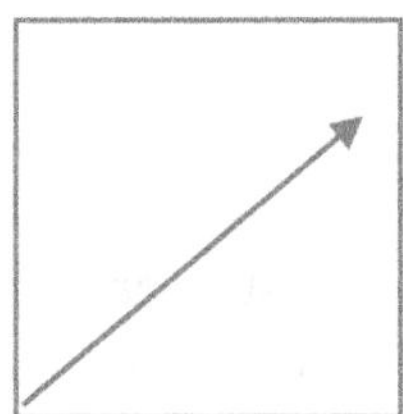

Make Money, Righteously

Be fair and generous in all monetary dealings.

Never cheat! Honesty is always required.

Your reputation as an honest businessperson is precious. Not only does it make you proud of your business, but it also is good business.

People obviously want to do business with other people that they trust. When customers are satisfied, they tend to buy again from the same vendor, and they tend to recommend that good vendor to their friends and relatives.

The marketplace, though, is fast moving, and there are too many unscrupulous characters. While bad actors eventually get found out and lose, they sow distrust throughout the market. This makes having an honest reputation even more valuable, because word of mouth that you are an honest vendor becomes even more highly valued by customers.

How you determine and communicate your pricing is a key manifestation of your business honesty. But business honesty goes beyond just pricing. How you build, deliver, and support your product also contributes to your business's fairness. Making your business good requires an attitude to be good in all aspects of your business.

Price Fairly

You shall have just balances, just weights, a just ephah, and a just hin.[90].

- *Leviticus* 19:35-36

The shopkeeper must wipe his measures twice a week, his weights once a week, and his scales after every weighing.

- *Talmud*

Honest weights and measures is taken very seriously in *Torah* and *Talmud*. Fair and honest pricing is compared in importance to honoring parents and kindness to animals.

When the *Talmud* was written commerce was comprised mostly of trade in local goods. Produce and grains were not pre-packaged, and wine was not pre-bottled. And currency was not as well regulated. So, no surprise that traditional fair pricing rules were written mostly in terms of local retail transactions, like measures for dry goods and liquid goods.

Today, expect your customers to comparison shop. Comparing prices is especially easy today given the Internet and social media.

If you are the low-cost provider it is a very significant advantage. However, compete only on price and you eventually will lose based upon price. Eventually someone will come along with a better production process or a substitute product that is cheaper. So, while being the low-cost provider is an enviable position, this is a difficult strategy to perpetuate.

There are at least two ways to help maintain your cost advantage.

> First, never forget that quality still is part of your customers' buying decision. Use your cost advantage to make incremental quality improvements to differentiate your offering.
>
> Second, increase your sales volume to generate further cost savings from economies of scale.
>
> However, carefully consider incremental costs that you would need to add to execute either of these strategies. (Remember

---

[90] An ancient Hebrew measure for liquid goods.

TANSTAAFL.) Increasing your fixed costs adds risk, because you would have to sell more to reach breakeven. The positive tradeoff is your profit margin should be greater above that breakeven point.

Generally, shy away from advertising that you are the low-cost provider. Your customers will figure out that your costs are attractive anyway. Rather, build up your reputation. Being the high-volume producer generates its own appeal, because customers tend to assume that the biggest provider must be doing something right.

If you are not the low-cost provider don't try to hide that fact. Again, customers will comparison shop. Rather, emphasize and be proud of your differentiation. This takes creativity. It usually involves identifying unique characteristics of your product that fit especially well with a particular market segment. Remember that differentiation can take many forms. Differentiation can be a product variation or the way you present, sell, and service your products.

Most importantly, you know whether your prices are fair. Don't be embarrassed to charge for your expertise and your time. Be transparent, if asked, to justify your pricing to a customer.

Talmud distinguishes between basic goods and luxury goods.

> *Profit on a basic good should be less than 1/6 the total cost.*
>
> \- *Talmud*

Profits on luxury items are not subject to this limitation. This ancient Jewish logic recognizes that people must buy a basic item, so its profit margin should be controlled. But a buyer does not have to purchase a luxury item, so the profits on luxury items are not controlled.

Talmud's guidance is generally consistent with modern economic theory. To the extent that essential goods are commodities, or similarly undifferentiated, a competitive economy will drive out any excess profits for these types of goods.

> *A middleman should not earn profit on life's essentials.*
>
> \- *Talmud*

The implication, here, is that a middleman doesn't add much value, so isn't entitled to much, if any, profit.

This ties to our earlier discussion about how the internet is replacing value that distributors previously provided. So, if you are in a middleman business strive to generate value-added, and make sure that both your supplier and customer appreciate the value you are adding.

Open competition is the favored model, although Talmud permits monopolistic businesses in some situations, such as utilities.

> *Talmud permits monopolistic businesses that are a clear benefit to society. But Talmudic rabbis recognized that these situations must be closely regulated to ensure that the benefits to the public remain real and that excess profits do not accrue to the monopolistic business.*
>
> \- Rabbi Jacob Blumenthal[91]

We expect our government to regulate such monopolies to prevent price gouging on such a basic good. We also expect our government to act to mitigate against any one country from gouging prices for a basic good, like petroleum.

> Oil is an unusual commodity, because oil supply depends upon the earth that you inhabit. It's not like livestock or other farming that can be copied on other lands. You either live atop oil, or you don't. Since *God* created the earth, including the oil that is in the earth, one person or one country should utilize those riches for the good of all peoples.
>
> Pharmaceuticals is a different sort of problem. Pharmaceuticals, mostly, are essential goods, but the cost to develop new drugs is very high and the payback period for a new drug is very long. There also is a lot of risk involved in developing new drugs, since many proposed new drugs do not make it all the way through clinical trials. Consequently, it is difficult for society to develop rules that balance the opposing objectives of controlling the cost of pharmaceuticals while allowing sufficient profit margins that provide sufficient incentive to develop new beneficial drugs.

Transparency is important to ensure honesty and to promote improvement. The Jewish stereotype of "I can get it for you wholesale" is not a fair description of wide-spread Jewish behavior.

---

[91] ExploringJudaism.org, "Talmudic Discussion on Monopolies"

Notice the difference between "bazaar" and "bizarre". A bazaar is a bunch of closely located small businesses peddling their goods in a very competitive marketplace. Bizarre is something kooky.

> Jews, Arabs, and some other cultures in Asia and Africa have flourishing marketplaces run as bazaars. In the Arab market in Jerusalem sellers go from complimenting you to cursing you out. This is part of the price setting process in that marketplace. Both the sellers and the buyers have fun in the process. Both the seller and the buyer want the other to be happy.
>
> Economically it is an efficient pricing model. The buyer pays according to his/her marginal willingness to pay, and the seller makes more sales while ensuring that the final prices are higher than the seller's cost.

If you are not used to shopping at a bazaar this behavior seems bizarre.

As business has shifted to larger stores, e.g. department stores and chain stores, and as sales have shifted to the Internet the opportunities to negotiate (haggle) prices has diminished. As a result, businesses must be more sophisticated in setting their prices, because on the spot price fine-tuning isn't as available.

Notice also that seasonal sales events can be counterproductive. Customers expect that these events will take place and wait for them. If most of your competitors are putting their goods on sale at the same time what is accomplished?

Good businesses learn to set their prices as optimally as practical. They must balance generating the most sales at prices enough above their cost to perpetuate their business. It's more complicated than just trying to maximize short term profits. It's also about developing a loyal, repeat customer base as well as reinvesting in the business.

Shop Fairly

> *Asking the price of an item if one has no intent to purchase it is forbidden. This is considered to harm the seller, getting his hopes up falsely.*
>
> *- Talmud*

We've been discussing how businesses, store owners and product distributors should compete fairly. And, we've discussed how the Internet has disrupted historical business structures, forcing more product and price transparency and lowering profit margins.

Now, let's talk about our role as consumers. Previously, we've also said that things happen in pairs. A product sale takes both a buyer and a seller. What is our ethical responsibility as buyers?

> A restaurant supply company in Philadelphia also carried appliances meant for sale for residences, including stove tops, ovens and dishwashers. Many shoppers came to their store, looked over the various models, and got price quotes. But these shoppers went home and compared prices from the Internet. Too often, these shoppers bought the same items on-line for only a little less.
>
> Was this fair? The restaurant supply company carried the cost burden of expensive inventory, and they spent personal time showing the various models to potential customers. The Internet Seller didn't have these same costs.
>
> After repeated frustrations of helping potential customers pick out the best appliance to fit their needs but losing the sale for seemingly minor price amounts, the restaurant supply company decided to discontinue sales to residences. Who missed out? Both the store and the shoppers lost value. The store lost incremental sales to residences. Residential shoppers no longer get personalized advice and the convenience of seeing the appliances in person.

This shopping behavior by consumers is common, and as we have discussed it is changing the landscape for retailing throughout America. Small retailers are being driven out of business. Consumers are enjoying lower prices, although perhaps consumers are getting less service, including personalized advice about product features and other choices.

As individual shoppers, ourselves, we have an ethical dilemma. We should utilize technology, such as the Internet, to make ourselves smarter shoppers. And we should take advantage of wider product choice and sometimes even faster delivery times by purchasing over the Internet. But, at the same time we should not unfairly take advantage of a local businessperson.

How should we do this? Frankly, our society is working this out. For example, our local bookstore now offers e-book sales. Customers can browse the bookshelves and get personalized recommendations from the store personnel. When it comes time to buy the store can deliver the book electronically. Behind the scenes, apparently, the giant on-line bookseller, Amazon, has amended their practices to pay a commission to the local bookseller. The bookstore probably earns a larger profit margin on paper-based books, but at least the store can accommodate customers who prefer reading their books on electronic devices.

Perhaps retailers should invite voluntary contributions for browsers who leave their store without a purchase and only with a better idea of what they want to buy. We're not used to voluntarily contributing to local retailers for their service, but we do routinely tip in restaurants.

As consumers, try to buy local when practical. Give the local store a chance to earn your business and enjoy the personal connection of knowing your local retailers.

Put It To Work

Asah (Do)

- Know your costs and reduce costs as much as practical.
- Know what your product sells for in the marketplace but get this information ethically.
- Welcome browsing in your store and try to make shoppers comfortable while they look around.
- Advertise sales to generate store traffic.
- Encourage your community to advertise "get it local" shopping days.

Bara (Create)

- Be transparent about your prices. Be willing to explain how you determined your price to any customer.
- Promote your overall sales by offering some items at reduced prices.

- Develop value-added packages, add-on products or services, that you can explain to potential customers and that, hopefully, your customers would value.
- Be aware that if you put items on sale each year at a predictable time, customers will wait for the sale. This might work to your benefit, even if it inevitably will depress sales just before the public expects to see your announced annual "sale".

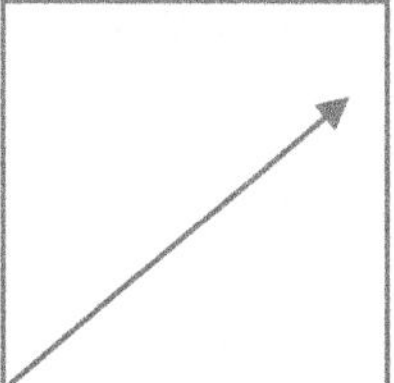

Time is Precious

Teach us to number our days so that we may get a heart of wisdom.

- *Psalms* 90:12

God created time! As far as we know, before the "Big Bang" there was no time. Also, as Einstein proved, time changes depending upon how fast we travel. Time is a dimension in which we can go forward but not backward. All these attributes of time are somewhat mysterious and spiritual.

Time is more precious than money.

- *Yiddish* saying

Our days are limited. Money that is lost may be regained, but time that is lost is lost forever.

We make choices all the time about how we spend our time. We all have very productive moments, and we all sometimes waste time.

Business can be all consuming. That can be an excess. We want and need time to reflect and replenish ourselves. We want and need time with our families.

Those of us who have worked in professional careers in which we billed by-the-hour may be more keenly aware of the value of our time. But all of us should understand that we can create more value for ourselves, just by utilizing our time more efficiently. Saved time can be available for better business activity or for more personal away-from-the-office pursuits.

Time flies! There is spiritual value to saving time. We have more time to create.

Focus Your Mind

When You Have a Lot To do, Go to Sleep

- *Yiddish* Saying

No doubt, you've witnessed people in the business community who seem to always be rushing, always late, and hassled about work. "I have so much to do" is their refrain.

And, you probably know people who are exceptionally productive and not overly stressed about their deadlines.

Putting aside that we each have a different personality makeup, very productive people seem to take work pressures more in stride. They embody the spirit of the *Yiddish* expression above.

You are where your mind is.

- Baal Shem Tov[92]

Sleep refreshes our bodies and our minds. When we dream our conscious and subconscious thoughts mix. We get inspired, even when we don't remember our dreams explicitly. Some people meditate effectively, and this practice similarly both relaxes and focuses their thoughts.

It's a matter of being present, really present, to concentrate on the matters at hand.

The most important thing is to remember the most important thing.

- Suzuki Roshi[93]

Your business plan should focus your attention. In your business plan you would have identified specific objectives for your business unit and have assigned accountabilities to managers within your business, including those key tasks that you, yourself, need to accomplish.

Ineffective management teams seem to jump from one emergency to another. This may be a symptom of not doing effective business planning

---

[92] Israel ben Eliezer (1698-1760), known as the *Baal Shem Tov*, was a Jewish mystic and is regarded as the founder of *Hasidic* Judaism.

[93] Suzuki Roshi (1904-1971) was a Zen Buddhist monk who helped popularize Zen Buddhism in the U.S. Many American Jews have been drawn to these studies, in part because some of those practices are similar to how Judaism teaches how to spiritually connect with nature.

or not paying attention to the business plan. If your organization seems to frenetically jump from one priority to another take this seriously. Fix your business plan. And concentrate your mind on those priorities that your business plan outlines.

Spiritual Time - Best Practices

> *When you need brains, brawn doesn't help.*
>
> - *Yiddish* saying

Being productive is a matter of working smart.

Observant Jews worship as a group three times each day: morning, afternoon, and evening. Essentially, they remind and redirect themselves towards *God*'s mission, do Good!

Jews also refresh and redirect their attention on a weekly, monthly and annual basis.

A key prayer during *Yom Kippur*[94] lists *Teshuvah*, *Tefillah*, and *Tzedakah* as key to improving our opportunity for a long and productive life.

> *Teshuvah*: Commonly translated as "repentance", but more accurately means "turn", as in turn away from past mistakes. Make amends for past mistakes and look forward to doing better. The future is a new opportunity.
>
> *Tefillah*: Commonly translated as "prayer" but encompasses joining together of "mind and spirit". We dedicate ourselves to be in union with *God*'s teachings. Be good!
>
> *Tzedakah*: Commonly translated as "charity", but truly reflects doing "acts of loving kindness". We don't seek reward for our acts. Rather, we act in pursuit of justice. Be righteous!

Businesses typically spend a lot of time planning and communicating internally with employees to get everyone on-the-same-page. Directing employees on the planned tactics for the coming period is important.

---

[94] *Unetanneh Tokef* prayer is attributed to Rabbi Amnon of Mainz, Germany about one thousand years ago. It translates approximately as "Let Us Speak of the Awesomeness". (Chabad.org)

But perhaps even more important is cultivating and motivating employees to understand and commit to the business' values. This can be a profound opportunity for your business.

Without literally utilizing *teshuvah*, *tefillah*, and *tzedakah* in a secular business setting, consider these as metaphoric lessons for business virtues which you should reinforce for your business teams.

> New Opportunities: The upcoming year is a new opportunity. Fix known business weaknesses without dwelling on the past. Build on business strengths but don't rest on laurels. Create a better business in the coming period. (*Teshuvah*)
>
> Teamwork and Purpose: We all want to do the right thing. Listen and help each other to continually make our business processes better. (*Tefillah*)
>
> Kindness Towards Each Customer: Treat each customer as we would want to be treated ourselves. Fix customer complaints (imperfections happen) even if it entails, within reason, some extra cost. Do it because it is the just thing to do for the customer. (*Tzedakah*)

Talking about values and motivating employees to act virtuously is difficult. It's less concrete than outlining, measuring, and rewarding tactical achievements.

But in the long run this kind of business spirituality contributes to success. As the CEO, or business leader for your unit, you cannot be involved in all decisions nor be aware of all business activities. You obviously should lead by example. Ultimately building a great company requires developing a business culture that shares its business values and develops its employees to act accordingly. This takes continuous reinforcement.

Boker Tov (Hebrew for "Good morning")

Your Wednesday is longer than your Thursday.

- *Yiddish* saying

Other proverbs convey a similar message. Time cannot be stored away, and so we shouldn't waste the current moments.

The business lesson, of course, is that daily time management is important. Tomorrow may bring another crisis.

We spend time each day, including at work, on seemingly non-essential matters, such as friendly sharing and discussions about current events. Of course, developing and maintaining personal relationships is important too. There also is value in team-building exercises which are organized and designed to develop familiarity and ease within work teams.

Balance is required. There is a time and place for discussing non-work matters.

When I was consulting, for example, I often managed cross-functional teams of consultants who had not worked together previously. We were put together to form a custom designed team focusing on our client's particular needs. After work and over dinner we got to know each other informally which was very useful to develop team rapport. But, during the workday each consultant was focused on completing their assigned project tasks.

It is not good for a man to be without knowledge, and he who makes haste with his feet misses his way.

- *Proverbs 19:2*

Rushing can be counterproductive.

When I was very young, I accompanied my father to work, and we were leaving the house very early before my sisters and mother were up. My father was hurrying me, and he said, "Move quickly, but not so fast that you make mistakes." Good advice. It worked.

You can find the time.

As consultants we occasionally were assigned pressing problems, such as when a company was acquiring another company, and they had a limited time to complete their due diligence. Our problem was we had other things going on with other clients. We couldn't drop our current client's project, nor could we put off doing the due diligence project. It required juggling multiple projects and working long hours. Somehow, we got it done and did a quality job.

You cannot keep up working much longer than normal hours. Everyone needs a break. - - - This is the brilliance of *Shabbat*, sabbath.

Employees should take vacations. Depending upon your business this may take special care to coordinate time-off for critical resources.

There are many tips for working efficiently. For example, when I became the Chief Actuary for an insurance company, I had many business papers to read. Some were important position papers very relevant to decisions for my company. I had to read those. Others seemed interesting and pertinent. I put them into the "B" pile to read when I got a spare moment. And, then there was the "C" pile, nice to read. Truth be told, I rarely got past the "A" pile, and when the other piles got too high, they went into the trash too.

Management Meetings

Management meetings are expensive.

> A one-hour meeting costs about 2.5% of a single person's time[95].
>
> Many meetings involve only two people. Group meetings typically involve 5 or more people. If five people attend a meeting each week, it's the equivalent of 10% of a headcount.
>
> If the salaries of the people attending are considered the cost of just a one-hour meeting with five people amounts to, at least, hundreds of dollars[96].

These costs skyrocket if many people attend a meeting, if there are

---

[95] One hour is 2.5% of a forty-hour work-week. (1/40 = 2.5%)

[96] If each attendee makes $100,000 per year their salary is about $50 per hour excluding benefits and overhead (assumes 2000 work hours per year). Adding in benefits and overhead (say 50%) comes to $75 per hour. Five people with these salary and benefit characteristics comes to $375 per hour.

multiple meetings each week, and if meetings extend to several hours each.

Management self-help guides coach that any meeting should follow simple steps, such as:

1. Define the Meeting Objectives. Have an agenda.
2. Create a set time to start and end and a space for the meeting. This can be in-person, but increasingly meetings take place virtually.
3. Invite the appropriate people.
4. Stay on track.
5. End the meeting with clear actions, owners, and timelines.

A lot of things don't need to be handled in a meeting setting. Can you accomplish the task without a meeting?

Meetings can be very useful, even essential, in running a business. After all, your business organization is supposed to accomplish things that one person cannot do as well by themselves. But most businesses have too many meetings. And meetings that should be very useful often are not well run, wasting time and money.

Business meetings generally fall into two types: sharing information or debating a topic. Having both objectives on the same agenda is problematic. Attendees often are not clear which is the purpose. Are they attending to gather information or to debate an issue?

Information sharing meetings are quite common. We have staff meetings, periodic all-hands briefings, cross-functional sharing meetings, project status check-up meetings, and so on.

Information sharing often doesn't have to take place face to face. If there needs to be a face-to-face meeting, the presentation highlights should be sent in advance. During the meeting, the presentation should be limited to expand on one or two important points or to answer questions. Attendees should be expected to read materials beforehand, so that it isn't necessary to re-read what was previously sent.

Meetings to debate a topic should be staged differently. The purpose of a debate meeting is to solicit opposing points of view and to gauge the degree of consensus that exists on a particular controversial topic. The conversation at the meeting should be designed so that attendees can briefly share their opinions. The actual decision may not be made at the meeting, since the manager responsible for the decision can take what was expressed under advisement and announce his/ her decision separately.

Attendees at debate meetings should feel that they are in a safe space, free to voice their opinions. As the leader of the meeting, you want to hear pros and cons.

If a decision topic were simple there really wouldn't be a need for a debate meeting.

> *It is possible to be passionate and still open to debate, to acknowledge the merit in other views and still believe they are wrong.*
>
> \- Rabbi David Wolpe[97]

The only boss is *God*. So, Jewish debate fleshes out pros and cons. When Jews disagree, the debate is temporarily adjourned. Then, each participant prays on the matter. They study rabbinic commentary that is relevant (e.g. *Talmud*). They ask *God* for guidance (prayer and meditation) to do the right thing. "What would *God* want us to do? What would accomplish the most Good?" Then, the attendees re-congregate to see how their thinking has changed after praying on the matter.

American businesses don't usually vote on debatable issues either. The CEO, or accountable manager, decides. The purpose of internal debate is to provide the CEO with pros and cons to inform their decision. If this is your situation, make it clear to attendees that a meeting debate is to provide input, but the manager will decide the matter.

When you do have a meeting keep it on schedule. That shows how you value your teammates time, as well as maximizing your own time. Establish a meeting culture that sticks to an agenda and sets timeframes. This takes discipline and practice. Once established the attendees at these meetings will appreciate how it honors everyones time, and they will

---

[97] Forward.com – July 22,2020

help to keep your meetings on track.

Metrics

You cannot improve what you don't measure.

- Peter Drucker[98]

Everyone likes to be complimented, and nobody wants to be reprimanded. Measures, therefore, that grade us are very powerful motivators. But, over emphasis on a particular measure, such as earnings per share, can mask the real objective.

Nevertheless, throughout our lives we are obsessed with measures.

> As very young children, our mother usually was the one who guided us. "Good boy!" "Don't do that again!"
>
> When we were a little older our father may have become the rewarder-in-chief or the disciplinarian, as the case may have been. "Just wait until your father gets home!"
>
> In school we responded to elaborate grading systems. We were graded on subject matter, work habits, and behavior. Later, we were given standardized tests that heavily influenced where we could attend school, and which subjects we were encouraged to study. ("SAT", "Achievement Tests")
>
> We took tests to get licensed in our chosen profession.
>
> In business, we grade ourselves ultimately by our company's stock price (at least for public companies). Stock prices correlate with a company's profitability, but not always very closely.[99]

Jews, no doubt, have done quite well throughout these testing regimes. However, Jewish wisdom is deeper than this testing mentality.

---

[98] Peter Drucker (1905-2005) was Jewish and a famous management consultant.

[99] Past profits do not necessarily predict future profitability. And, accounting anomalies can impact current reported profitability.

The underlying Jewish motivation is . . .

> *When you live by the absolute standards of an omniscient God, you need to be the best you can possibly be.*
>
> - Tzvi Freeman[100]

The words "absolute" and "omniscient" in this quote might be troublesome for you. There are decisions that are not clear-cut, such that good people might disagree. The wise Jew always tries to do *good*, although two Jews may argue about which choice is the most good. As for omniscient, the wise Jew acts as if *God* is watching, but wise Jews may think that "watching" personifies *God* too much. But the quote is okay as metaphor; it urges us to always try to do better.

Excellence goes beyond simple measures. To the extent that a measure is relevant at all, its purpose is to benchmark your individual achievement to give you a new target to strive to beat. Just beating the other guy, or the competitor, is not good enough. If the other guy or competitor is not good, what does it mean to beat their performance by a little bit?

Bottom line: Doing good, developing customer satisfaction, and continual improvement are worthy objectives. Develop metrics for your company that focuses attention on what really counts.

Look Forward

> *The eggs think they're smarter than the chickens.*
>
> - *Yiddish* saying

There are <u>*leading*</u> indicators and <u>*lagging*</u> indicators.

In businesspeople obsess about financial results, but the problem is that these inherently are lagging indicators. In fact, public companies are very careful to qualify any statements they make about their future prospects. You hear the phrase, "Past results are not necessarily indicative of future results". Accounting statements do have the advantages of being promptly available at the end of each calendar quarter, and financial

---

[100] Chabad.org, "Jewish Guilt"

statements can be readily compared across companies.

But what you really want to know are leading indicators like:

> What new products are in the pipeline?
>
> What percentage of finished goods need to get trashed or repaired to meet good quality standards? Is the company improving in this regard?
>
> How do a company's key customers feel about the service they are getting from the company?
>
> Does the company have the appropriate talent and bench-strength to fill key positions within the company? How do the employees feel about working for that company?

There also are *individual* and *team* measures. A well-run business wants to measure and assess their objectives overall. But also, each department or work team wants to measure an assess these types of objectives.

This brings us to *objective* versus *subjective* measures. Objective measures are usually easier to measure and gauge. Nevertheless, you don't want to get too bogged down in collecting these measures. Also, key objective measures that are most relevant to the company's goals may change from year to year. Your goal is to isolate a few objective leading indicators that are most meaningful.

Subjective measures also may be very relevant, but they often are harder to measure and assess. For example, you can ask a customer if they feel satisfied with their purchase. You may even ask the customer to give you a numeric score, such as on a scale from 1 to 10, how satisfied are you with our product? But, two different customers could experience the same thing, and yet have different degrees of satisfaction.

Survey techniques try to minimize these measurement problems by collecting a sufficiently large sample of replies and comparing the results over time to assess whether attitudes are shifting.

Break-down complicated projects into smaller steps.

> *And I have come down to deliver them out of the hand of the Egyptians, and to bring them up out of that land to a good and broad land, a land flowing with milk and honey.*
>
> \- *Exodus* 3:8

Moses' project was very complicated. Getting to the *Promised Land* took many steps. It took forty years with many obstacles along the way. Of course, *God* was guiding Moses.

Many important business projects necessarily span multiple years or involve multiple disciplines, and complications can be expected to occur along the way. Technology implementation projects, for example, frequently take longer and cost more than anticipated. Similarly, business expansion projects usually entail many complications. Even hiring a new key employee may present surprises and setbacks.

Progress is a long process. Recognize this up-front. Breakdown major projects into smaller steps with interim milestones. Also, recognize that redirecting peoples' skills has its own complications. Motivating, retraining, and supporting employees and managers who are given responsibility for large projects requires special attention.

"Scope creep" is common. People involved in a major project may change their minds about what they recommended at an earlier stage in the project. Obviously, there are situations where a project's scope needs amending. But open-ended changes in scope often doom a project. Interim milestones are helpful to keep a project on track as well as to focus attention on the ultimate goals for a major project.

Put It To Work

Asah (Do)

- Distinguish between information meetings and debate meetings.
- Choose attendees selectively and make them aware of the purpose of each meeting.
- Send briefing materials and expect participants to read the materials

before the meeting.

- Start and end meetings on time.
- At the end of a meeting assign expectations for next steps including who is accountable for those steps.
- List and rank the key projects that you plan for your business over the next month, quarter, and year.
- Decide measures that are relevant and important to gauge how well you are meeting your business objectives.
- Measure and communicate progress on key projects.
- Be frank and prompt when a project is not going according to plan.

Bara (Create)

- Be aware of what time of the day that you are most productive and schedule yourself accordingly.
- Let people manage their own personal time, as long as they realize their accountabilities.
- Communicate both your annual and long-range plans internally. Use these to generate enthusiasm.
- Discuss results. Analyze what might be causing trends in the results.
- Get buy-in for key projects.
- If you have difficulty getting your important work done something is out of whack. Make adjustments, and if necessary, get assistance[101].

[101] coursera.org ,"Work Smarter, Not Harder: Time Management for Personal & Professional Productivity"

Manage Your Money, Wisely

> *Money makes the world go around*
> *The world go around; The world go around*
> *Money makes the world go around*
> *It makes the world go 'round."*

- Performed by Joel Grey, Jewish entertainer.[102]

Why do you want money?

First, you need to provide for yourself and your family. You want enough money to get by and then some to enjoy life.

Part of caring for your family is saving for your own retirement. You pray to be healthy and spend quality time with your spouse, children and grandchildren. You also want to enjoy other pursuits such as hobbies or charity work.

Torah teaches that you should give time and money to charity, not just in retirement.

> *For the poor will never cease out of the land; therefore I command you. You shall open wide your hand to your brother and to the poor in the land.*

- *Deuteronomy* 15:11

You want to leave a memorable legacy to your children, including financial assets. But even more importantly, you want to leave a better world.

[102] From "Cabaret", Broadway musical. John_Kander and Fred Ebb, Composer and Lyricist, were among the many Jewish Broadway songsters.

Your Life's Portfolio

Who is rich? He who rejoices in his portion.

- Talmud

Your portfolio is a collection of parts, and you want the whole to be more than the sum of those parts. You want the parts to work together to accomplish your goals.

You will make investment decisions throughout your life, and some of the most important investment decisions don't involve the stock market. Among life's very important decisions are what occupation will you pursue; when and whom will you marry; how many children will you have; where will you chose to reside; and how will you fill your leisure time. You don't think of these as investment decisions. And, truly, these are not decisions in which money should be a primary concern. But, nevertheless, these decisions are choices that involve dedicating major portions of your attention.

As a child and extending into your teenage years, you may not have thought much about money. Hopefully, your family was well-enough off to provide for your basic needs during those formative years.

If your family was poor when you were a child, no doubt you were made aware of the family's financial situation. You shared in your family's struggles.

If your family was especially wealthy when you were a child hopefully your parents taught you the responsibilities that go with great wealth.

In our 20's and 30's it's understandable that money is often forefront in our thinking as careers are just starting. A young growing family faces relatively higher needs for money as they start their household and provide for their young children.

In our 40's, 50's and 60's typically we reach our peak earnings years. We tend to focus on saving for retirement. And we tend to give relatively more to charity.

Some people are lucky to visualize for themselves a lifelong purpose.

Among the fellow inmates in the concentration camp, those who survived were able to connect with a purpose in life to feel

> *positive about and who then immersed themselves in imagining that purpose in their own way, such as conversing with an (imagined) loved one.*
>
> - Victor Frankl[103]

Frankl's horrible experiences in a Concentration Camp and his subsequent study of psychotherapy showed how fundamental it is to feel a purpose for one's life.

Many people are fortunate to identify a career direction that provides a sense of meaningfulness to their work. Others find purpose outside of work raising children, helping a charity, teaching or coaching, writing or creating art, or other pursuits.

Be clear about your business' purpose. Continue to test with your customers how well they perceive that your business fulfills that purpose. This will not only focus your company's plans, but it should help to provide meaningfulness for your employees.

Risk

> *The best choice of a portfolio is one that minimizes risk for a given expected return.*
>
> - Harry Markowitz[104]

We've discussed the fundamental Jewish wisdom that only *God* is perfec[t.] The flip side is: The world is not perfect. And so, things don't necessarily turn out as we would expect.

> *Sometimes you win; Sometimes you lose; Sometimes it rains.*
>
> - Ron Shelton[105]

---

[103] Victor Frankl, Man's Search for Meaning, 1946. Frankl was a Holocaust survivor who was imprisoned in a concentration camp. His book recounted his experiences and outlined what became known as "Logotherapy", a psychological therapy.

[104] Harry Markowitz (1927 - 2023) was known as the Father of Modern Portfolio Theory. He won the Nobel Prize in economics in 1990.

[105] Shelton wrote and directed the movie "Bull Durham", a film about baseball. In baseball even the best teams lose and the best players strike out a relatively large percentage of the opportunities.

There is risk in everything. (See "Man Plans and God Laughs")

"Risk" is the idea that a future outcome may not come out as expected.

Harry Markowitz changed traditional thinking about investments. Prior to 1952 when Harry published his first study, the standard thinking was buy shares in a group of companies that were thought to have the best prospects. Harry upended that thinking, showing that wasn't necessarily the best investment strategy.

Harry showed that there is a tradeoff between risk and return. In other words, to get a higher expected return it's necessary to accept more risk.

> Sam owns stock in "A" Company, and Ira owns stock in "B" Company. Both Company A and Company B are projected to return 7% over the next year, but the history of Company B shows that their historical results have been more volatile from year to year. Which is the better stock? Answer: Probably Company A. Ira should sell Company B and buy Company A to get same expected return for less risk.
>
> Marvin joins his friends, Sam and Ira, and Marvin touts a stock, "C" Company. Marvin says that C is projected to earn 10% next year.
>
> Should Sam and Ira buy C Company? Not necessarily. C Company should earn more, but it may have much more risk, meaning that it also has a higher chance of losing money.

Every investment has two sides. An investor, who puts money into a deal, expects the money to be tied up for a while, but nevertheless expects to get back more than they put in. Whomever takes the money plans to put it to use and earn more than they must pay back to the investor. Both sides think they are getting a good deal.

But obviously it doesn't always work out well. Many investments don't make as much as anticipated. Some investments lose money. This is because humans make mistakes. Businesses, even those that are very well run and well planned, don't always win.

Investments, like any business deal, may lose money. There is no sure thing - no risk-free investment.[106]

Financial experts teach that the most important "manage money" decision is how much risk to take. Think twice about taking any more risk than you need. And don't take so much risk that you are uncomfortable.

Other financial coaches often espouse some investing rules-of-thumb, two of the most common "rules" are:

> Subtract your age from 100. Keep that percentage of your overall liquid assets in fixed investments, rather than equities.

> When you retire only take out 4% of your overall assets each year.

These are only guidelines, approximations. They presume that fixed income investments are less risky than equity investments. And they presume that current interest rates are not going to change much.

When interest rates are changing significantly, up or down, these rules of thumb are not necessarily optimum.

Risk and return go hand in hand. More accurately, risk and *expected* return go hand-in-hand. A higher *expected* return very likely entails more risk, which means that there is relatively more chance of underperforming expectation.

Outperforming the Market

It's not how much you earn; it's how much you keep.

- Yiddish saying

Is it possible to outperform the market? Yes and No.

Some investments have done very well. Their track record shows that they beat the market. But will they continue to beat the market?

---

[106] U.S. Treasury bonds and FDIC insured bank CD's are almost risk free. They are guaranteed by the U.S. Government. But who knows? They are not guaranteed by God.

Past success does not guarantee future success. Companies that have done well in the recent past are perceived to have positive momentum ("momentum" stocks), and excellent companies should be able to build upon their strengths.

Some companies have knowledge that is not available to the general marketplace, and based upon their unique knowledge they should be able to continue to outperform. For example:

> A small, family business may have institutional knowledge, such as supplier contacts, experienced staff, a desirable location, and a good local reputation. These strengths have been earned by these businesses over time through their own creativity and hard work. Based upon their hard-earned strengths they may be enabled to continue to outperform in their small business niche.
>
> An entrepreneur may have a unique, new invention or new process that promises to make their business venture beat the existing competition.

But we're talking probabilities here. Just because a company has done well in the past, doesn't mean that it definitely will outperform in the future. Something unforeseen may upset the apple cart.

Even after the fact, it is sometimes difficult to discern whether that company's success was brilliantly earned or random.

In a "A Random Walk Down Wall Street[107]" by Burton Malkiel argues that picking individual public stocks is foolhardy, and there is lots of scholarship and research that backs up Dr. Malkiel's thesis. Jeremy Siegel[108], another brilliant Jewish financial scholar, has tested Malkiel's thesis and advises that it is more efficient to invest in mutual funds or indexes that reflect large sections of the overall marketplace.

Nevertheless, picking individual stocks to try to outperform the marketplace is very tempting, and you will have much company (no pun

---

[107] Dr. Burton Malkiel, A Random Walk Down Wall Street, 1973. Malkiel is a professor of economics at Princeton University. There are over 2 million copies in print, and this book has been called "one of the few great investment books".

[108] Jeremy Siegel, Stocks for the Long Run, McGraw Hill, October 2022. Siegel is a Finance Professor at Wharton School of University of Pennsylvania.

intended) if you are among the investors that try to do this. We hear about, and are jealous of, the tremendous success of companies like *Microsoft*, *Amazon*, *Google*, *Amazon*, and *Tesla*. After the fact, it's clear these companies developed something special. In these companies' earliest stages, it was not so obvious that they would be so successful. We tend not to hear about the many, many technology and other ventures that went bust before their product made it to market or fizzled when their products were not successful.

When selecting an individual stock investment do your research. Understand the company's strategy, their internal financial strength, their particular risks. Be very leery of salespeople touting that they "know" this particular company will be a winner.

In business you also will be confronted with lots of opportunities, and the salespeople (hawking a new business venture, a publicly traded stock, some other investment, even a politician with a new idea) will argue that their opportunity is different. In effect, these salespeople are arguing that they have inside knowledge. They argue: "Their investment will beat the market".

So, beating the market depends upon having superior knowledge. It's possible, especially through hard work, due diligence, and training to gather knowledge that may give you special insight.

But don't be fooled by recent success nor by a good story.

Even the most astute investors don't win every time.

Even a well thought out business plan with very good people doesn't necessarily win every time.

All investments have risk. All businesses have risk.

Interest

When you come into the land and plant all kinds of trees for food, then you shall count their fruit as forbidden, three years it shall be forbidden for you, it must not be eaten. And in the fourth year all their fruit shall be holy, an offering of praise to the Lord. But in the fifth year may you eat of their fruit, that they yield more richly for you. I am the Lord your God.

- *Leviticus* 19:23-25

Would you rather have $100 now or a promise to receive $100 one year from now? Answer: Now. Money on-hand now is more valuable than money promised to you later. We call this the *time value of money*.

"Interest" is the cost that the lender requires the borrower to pay, and the amount of interest depends upon several factors.

Interest rates are determined in the financial marketplace, essentially by negotiation. Lenders or investors offer money at terms they desire, and borrowers seek to get the best deal.

Several considerations influence the interest rate at which a lender would agree to issue a loan. These factors are not displayed, nor necessarily calculated separately. But these influences typically are what determines the interest rate for a particular loan.

(1) *Risk free rate:* Money, in hand, is always worth more than money down the road. Money in hand gives you the opportunity to invest in something better.

(2) *Expected Inflation:* Inflation in a growing economy is usually positive. The giver of a loan expects to be paid for tying up their money for the duration of the loan, because the purchasing power of their dollars that they will get back at the end of the loan will be less due to inflation.

(3) *Interest rate risk*: Longer loans usually require higher interest rates, because lenders want to be compensated more if inflation increases.

(4) *Default Risk*: A lender won't lend to a borrower whom they perceive cannot pay back the loan, and a lender will charge a higher interest rate to a borrower whom the lender perceives is relatively more likely to default.

Present Value

> *Therefore its name was called Ba'bel, because there the Lord confused the language of all the earth, and from there the Lord scattered them abroad over the face of all the earth.*
>
> \- *Genesis* 11:9

People view things differently and describe them differently.

Even with perfect information different people may make differing decisions about a particular investment. There are other values involved besides money. And each person's attitudes about risk vary.

That doesn't stop financial analysts though, from trying to boil down the comparison of alternative investments to simple numerical calculations. While well-meaning, such characterizations of investments may be over-simplifications and cause confusion among untrained investors.

Keeping in mind this caveat, some simplified measures for comparing alternative investments can be useful.

Present value is the equivalent dollar amount that represents all the prospective cash flows expected from a particular investment. Generally speaking, you would be willing to pay this single amount (present value) for the investment.

> When you borrow money, say for a mortgage, the amount you borrow is the present value of the loan. You are committing to a series of principal and interest payments over time, say monthly, and the lender expects to receive that periodic flow of payments.
>
> When you invest, say buy a company's stock, you essentially are projecting to receive over time periodic dividend payments, and you expect that in the future you or your heirs will sell the stock. The amount you pay now for the stock is its present value. The amount you will get back is a long series of expected payments, and you are not sure how much exactly you will get back or when.

When your business contemplates a particular strategy, it implicitly projects a series of outputs and inputs. A business outlays funds over time (e.g. buying raw materials and paying salaries). These outlays of funds don't usually correspond to when a business may expect to take funds out of the business (e.g. dividends or return of profits to investors).

Both the outflows and the inflows of money are projections, estimates. Nevertheless, the business makes best estimates of all these flows of money related to the proposed strategy. There usually is more certainty estimating the outflows. The level and timing of the inflows of money may be very uncertain.

Suppose your business is considering two, or more, variations of a proposed strategy. For example, launch two products simultaneously; advertise a little or a lot; or launch in alternative territories. How does the business compare these alternatives?

Present value can be calculated for any alternative scenario of periodic outlays and inflows of money. Generally, the alternative with the highest present value is better.

> "Discount rate" is similar to "interest rate". A business discounts future flows of money (outlays and inputs) using their "discount rate". (The discount rate can be thought of as the business' cost of money.)
>
> In situations where the initial amount of investment is known and the outlays and inputs of money are projected, the financial analyst can calculate an "Internal Rate of Return (IRR)". (The IRR can be thought of as the discount rate that would result in a specified amount of initial investment.)

Utility Value

Humans, generally, favor certainty. We don't like to take big risks.

But there are exceptions. Some people are more risk adverse than others. Yet, almost all of us, at some point in our lives, make relatively riskier choices. We make a choice that has attractive "utility value" to us, even though that particular choice may not have attractive "present value".

Here is an example. At your synagogue (or church or favorite charity) there is an event at which they are selling 50/50 raffle tickets. You understand that 50% of the raffle ticket sales will benefit the synagogue, and the other 50% will go to one winner. Purely from a *present value* point of view, you wouldn't buy such a raffle ticket, but in this situation, you happily buy some tickets. Why?

> Say you buy $10 worth of raffle tickets. The *present value* of the raffle tickets is only $5. You've given $5 worth of charity to your synagogue. The good feeling you get by giving charity is a benefit to you. (Jews say using *Yiddish*, "You get *naches*", which is *Yiddish* meaning "joy". Financial nerds would say, you get *utility value* when you give to charity.)
>
> You have a chance to win the raffle, and if you are the winner, you will get back much more than the $10 that you paid for the raffle tickets. That is a thrill. The thrill, chance of winning big, provides additional *utility value* to you.

Your personal situation may alter the *utility value* of a business choice. For example, you just got married, or you are expecting a baby. Suddenly you perceive greater responsibilities, so that your perceived need for money is greater. You may be more inclined to change jobs. Or you feel more need to work harder; put in extra time at work; take extra courses to advance your career.

In these situations, your perceived need for money has changed. Money now has more *utility value* to you.

Your perceived need for money also may decrease for logical reasons. When you retire you give up earning potential. Hopefully, you've saved sufficiently over the years to take care of yourself, your spouse, and dependent children. You may no longer have a mortgage on your home.

Utility value refers to how much you perceive a need for money. Your *utility valu*e for money is personal. Your situation impacts your *utility value* for money, but you are unique. Your personal need for money and the timing of when you need money varies from others.

Don't confuse *utility value* with risk. *Utility value* reflects how much you want or need money. Risk, on the other hand, is inherent in each particular business or investment alternative.

Financial Leverage

Give me a lever and a place to stand and I will move the earth.
- Archimedes[109]

When Sarah died Abraham purchased the *Cave of Machpelah*[110] to be the burial site for his family. Land ownership was the lever that bestowed acceptance for his family. This was well before the modern nation-state, and so "citizenship" as we know it did not exist. Land ownership established "I belong here".

In physics a lever makes it easier to move another object. A lever needs a fulcrum, a spot upon which the lever pivots.

Jewish wisdom is like a lever which multiples your ability to make good business decisions. The fulcrum in Jewish wisdom is *Torah*, which is the ongoing interpretation of how *God* wants us to act.

In finance, "leverage" refers to borrowing money to invest more money. Financial leverage gives you the ability to multiply the total amount of investment you may make.

Financial leverage can be good or bad. If your investment is good, financial leverage will increase your financial return. If your investment is bad, financial leverage will increase your loss.

People and businesses commonly use financial leverage. When you get a mortgage to buy a house you are using financial leverage. If the value of the house goes up, then you will enjoy larger returns when you sell the house.

> Say, you put down 20% of the purchase price of a house. The house costs $400,000[111]. Your cash outlay, excluding settlement costs, would be $80,000. Suppose five years later you sell the house for

[109] Archimedes (287-212 BCE). Archimedes was a Greek mathematician. This is one of the few non-Jewish quotes in this book. (Jewish culture and Greek culture existed together during this time period.)
[110] *Exodus* 23:1-2. *Machpelah* is a series of caves about 30 kilometers south of Jerusalem.
[111] Median home price in 2023 in the U.S. was $428,000.

> $500,000.[112] The profit on sale of the home would be $100,000. But your outlay was only $80,000. Your profit percentage was 125%. (Your annual rate of return was slightly more than 9%, much better than the increase in the value of the home each year of 5%.)

Businesses borrow money when they sell stock in their company. Businesses also often borrow money ("corporate bonds"), which is advantageous to the business when their cost of borrowing is less than the rate of return, they plan to earn for their shareholders.

A business, and you, are limited in the amount of money you can borrow. Whoever lends money wants to be assured, as much as can be expected, that the business will put the borrowed money to good use.

> "Debt to equity" (ratio of total money *owed* to total money *owned*) measures the degree of financial leverage of a business. Depending upon the industry there are rules of thumb for how much debt/equity is considered heavy, making the investment in that company seem overly risky.

Financial leverage always increases risk. When an investment return is positive, financial leverage multiplies the profit for the borrower. But, if an investment loses money overall, the loss to the borrower is multiplied (remember: *TANSTAAFL*).

When an investment goes sour it's usually best to cut your losses. Investing more money, by itself, doesn't make a bad investment a good one. The expression is "throwing good money after bad." With more financial leverage things can get very bad very fast.

Taxes

> *Jewish law is clear about the obligation to obey the law and pay taxes. The Hebrew text is "dina malchuta dina" which means "the law of the land is the law".*
>
> \- *Talmud*[113]

[112] 5 percent annual inflation in value of home would result in value after 5 years of approximately $510,000.

[113] *Talmud: Bava Kamma* 113a

Nobody likes to pay taxes. We pay taxes, because we recognize that some things are better provided by our government. Moreover, we obey the laws of the land in which we live.

Taxes need to be fair. Otherwise, the populace will revolt in some way against what they perceive to be unfair taxes. (Voting to elect new government officials is our right in a democracy. Disobeying current law is not okay.)

Jewish law recognizes that different societies may make varying conclusions about the amount of tax and the means of distributing the tax paying burden. Taxes may be relatively uniform by person or progressive, varying based upon the ability to pay.

Based upon the tax laws of the land various investment alternatives may present themselves. For example, in the U.S. there are enticements in tax law to save for retirement, utilizing IRA, 401k, and similarly lawful investment vehicles. There also are varying tax treatments based upon how long an investment is held, short-term versus long-term capital gains, where the incentives favor holding investments longer.

Governments typically make allowances in tax law in favor of owning your own home.

Governments more and more make tax laws favoring investing in environmentally beneficial alternatives, such as EV autos, home energy efficiency improvements, etc.

Generally, good investments are good even though they result in taxes. However, bad investments don't turn good just because there are tax offsets.

So, when making a particular investment consider alternatives that legally minimize the tax consequences for you. Tax efficient alternatives may increase your expected return (i.e. make a positive expected return somewhat more positive).

Tax laws can be complex, and they change frequently. Determining the optimum tax efficient means for various investments is beyond our scope here. Consult a tax advisor when appropriate.

Ethical Investments

Words should be weighed, not counted.

- *Yiddish* saying

Jews have played important roles in money lending since the Middle Ages, if not earlier. In the Middle Ages Jews were not permitted to own land or engage in other types of commerce. And the Catholic church at that time did not permit its followers to charge interest on loans[114]. Lending became a way for some Jews to provide for their families while serving the wider economy by providing a necessary service.

Unfortunately, this also led to the stereotype that Jews committed usury since at that time some considered charging any rate of interest to be sinful.

Today most people recognize that loans, such as for mortgages and automobile purchases, are necessary services in our economy. Investors, including retirees, depend upon corporate and government bonds to provide retirement income. Businesses require loans to expand their business.

Still, there are many limitations and regulations surrounding money lending. State law in the U.S., for example, sets maximum interest rates for consumer debt. Financial disclosures for mortgages are regulated by the U.S Federal government.

Talmud has many guidelines concerning money lending, with fairness and kindness at the heart of all these guidelines. *Talmud* particularly provides guidelines for lending money to family and to the poor. And contrary to anti-Semitic slurs, *Talmud* also prohibits usury, which is charging too much interest for loans.

If you lend money to any of my people with you who is poor, you shall not be to him as a creditor, and you shall not exact interest from him.

- *Exodus* 22:25

[114] The Fifth Lateran Council in 1517 reversed the church's earlier prohibitions against charging interest on loans. (uscatholic.org, "Is it sinful to charge interest on a loan?")

It's okay to lend money to a family member, but *Torah* prohibits charging them interest. The wisdom here is to avoid or limit lending money to a family member unless that family member really needs the loan. And, in those situations lend the money without interest as a kindness.

> *When you reap the harvest of your land, you shall not reap your field to its very border, neither shall you gather the gleanings after your harvest. And you shall not strip your vineyard bare, neither shall you gather the fallen grapes of your vineyard; you shall leave them for the poor and the sojourner. I am the Lord your God.*
>
> \- *Leviticus* 19: 9-10

Torah explicitly directs Jews to give to the poor. Farmers, who let's remember was the predominant occupation in the time of the Bible, should leave the edges of their fields unharvested so that the poor could gather food themselves.

Maimonides, one of Judaism's greatest sages, commentary ranked the forms of charity.

> *The greatest form of charity is to train a poor person a skill so that they can support themselves.*
>
> *The second greatest form of charity is to give anonymously, so that neither the giver nor the receiver are aware of the other.*

Judaism does permit charging interest on a loan to a third party, one who is not a family member nor a poor person. Giving a loan extends benefit to the borrower as long as the loan is fair.

> *To a foreigner you may lend upon interest, but to your brother you shall not lend upon interest.*
>
> \- *Deuteronomy* 23:20

"Usury", charging too much interest, is never allowed. A lender should not take advantage of any borrower. There is always the following Jewish doctrine from Leviticus and referred to by Hillel, a great Jewish rabbi, as the essence of *Torah*.

Do Not Do To Others That Which You Would Find Hateful To Yourself.

- Hillel, Jewish leader and scholar; died 10 CE

Put It To Work

Asah (Do)

- Always be aware of TANSTAAFL. If an investment or business venture seems to good to be true, don't believe it.

- Expect to pay interest when you borrow money.

- Don't make any investment that you do not understand. Get a financial advisor to assist you. If you have a financial advisor, communicate clearly with him or her what are your specific and upcoming needs for money.

- Always obey tax laws. Always obey the law of the land.

Bara (Create)

- Know yourself. What are your needs for money? What gives you more utility value?

- Know your appetite for risk. Resist the temptation to invest in riskier investments, if the volatility of those investments will make you especially nervous.

- Don't just go by "gut feel". Write down your assumptions.

- Use financial leverage knowingly. If the investment, overall, is positive, financial leverage will increase your profit. If the investment, overall, is unprofitable, financial leverage will increase your loss.

- Taxation considerations never offset what otherwise is a poor investment. So, never make an investment solely based upon promises of tax advantages.

- When in doubt about the ethics of any deal, ask yourself, "What would God want me to do in this situation?"

Part 4 – Graduation Plans

Work for a Better Tomorrow

Be careful to heed all these words which I command you, that it may go well with you and with your children after you forever, when you do what is good and right in the sight of the Lord your God."

- *Deuteronomy* 12:28

The human gift of intelligence gives us the privilege and responsibility to think about tomorrow. This is divine. All animals innately care for their young, as that is built into nature. But, as far as we know, only humans think about the generations before them and to come after them.

We are keenly aware of our ethnic heritage.

Honor your father and your mother, that your days may be long in the land which the Lord your God gives you.

- *Exodus* 20:12

We cherish Jewish traditions, and we pass along our traditions to our children. Jewish traditions reflect wisdom accumulated over thousands of years.

We want our children to be more successful than ourselves. We admire our own parents hard work, and we provide as best we can for our children. We admire people who do good, as we endeavor to do good ourselves, and as we guide our children to do good.

But we don't define success merely in financial terms.

Who is rich? He who is happy with his lot.

- *Talmud*

Clean Up After Yourself

Then God said, "Let us make man in our image, after our likeness, and let them have dominion over the fish of the sea, and over the birds of the air, and over the cattle, and over the earth, and over every creeping thing that creeps upon the earth."

- *Genesis* 1:26

Torah established the moral foundation for ecology, even though the word "ecology" wasn't used[115] until the 19th century.

This verse, unfortunately, is often misunderstood. It doesn't mean that humans physically look like *God*. In fact, traditional Jews refrain from artwork depicting *God*, following this instruction from Deuteronomy.

You shall not make for yourself a graven image, or any likeness of anything that is in heaven above, or that is on the earth beneath, or that is in the water under the earth.

- *Deuteronomy* 5:8

Moses literally could not see *God* on Mount Sinai.

Moses said "I pray thee, show me thy glory"

But, he said "You cannot see my face, for man may not see me and live."

-*Exodus* 33:18 and 20

God instructed Moses to go into a cleft in the rocks, and *God* shielded his image from Moses. Moses saw *God*'s back, which the commentary says refers to traces of the divine Presence, the afterglow of God's supernatural radiance.[116]

So, what does it mean that humans were created as a likeness to *God*? What does it mean that humans shall rule the creatures in the world?

---

[115] "E*cology"*, the branch of science dealing with the relationship of living things to their environments was coined by German zoologist Ernst Haeckel in 1873.

[116] Etz Hayim Torah and Commentary - footnote to Exodus 20:23.

Humans have *dominion* ("rule") over the animals and plants, but we cannot *dominate* them. Our role is to take care of the earth and all of *God*'s creation. Preserve life. Improve things, so that *God*'s creations, including humankind, thrives. That's ecology!

When we think of ecology we usually think of species of plants and animals, depletion of natural resources, pollution, climate change, and other influences that we have on the earth and life on earth.

When we think of cleaning up after ourselves, we usually think of daily and weekly chores. We tell our children to make their beds and straighten their room. Someone in the household takes out the trash; washes the dishes; cleans the house. To keep our property nice, we make sure that snow is shoveled, leaves are raked, weeds are tended, windows are washed, and so on.

See the connections between ecology and cleaning. Daily, weekly, and seasonal cleaning connects with generational caring for all life and creation.

Your daily cleaning habits and your attention to ecology also connect to your business environment. Other people, likely, work in the same work area as you. Moreover, your own work in the long run will be more efficient if you have the right tools, a clean workspace, and organized work processes.

All these activities are connected. They are all *God* -inspired, or should be, and would be, if you start to think of these connections - to each other and to *God*.

Then, these chores and constraints cease to be hindrances. Instead, you will be inspired, and you will inspire others.

Lashon Hara (Evil Tongue) Happens

Rather a slip of the foot than a slip of the tongue.

- *Talmud*[117]

The *Talmud* calls derogatory speech about another person *lashon hara*,

[117] *Talmud: Ben Sira* 20:18

which is Hebrew meaning "evil tongue". *S*uch talk is forbidden even if the speech is truthful. The rabbis emphasize *lashon hara* in their teachings, because it is so hard for a person negatively described to overcome adverse word-of-mouth. *Lashon hara* also is emphasized, because this transgression is so common.

There is an old Chasidic tale[118] that illustrates the difficulty of *lashon hara.*

> A local businessman complained to his rabbi that a customer, let's call him Morty, was unhappy and was complaining about the situation all over town.
>
> The rabbi summoned Morty to speak with him. When they met, the rabbi asked Morty, "Do you have any feather pillows in your house?" Morty replied "Yes". And the rabbi asked Morty, "Please, bring me one."
>
> Morty was mystified, but he returned a bit later to the rabbi's study with a nice fluffy pillow under his arm. The rabbi opened the window and handed him a knife. "Cut it open!"
>
> "But Rabbi, it will make a mess!"
>
> "Do as I say!"
>
> Morty cut the pillow, and a cloud of feathers came out. They landed all over the rabbi's study, and a lot of them flew out of the window.
>
> The rabbi waited a few minutes, and then ordered, "Now bring me back all the feathers, and stuff them back in your pillow."
>
> Morty stared at the rabbi in disbelief. "That is impossible, Rabbi. The ones here in the room I might get, most of them, but the ones that flew out of the window are gone. Rabbi, I can't do that, you know it!"
>
> "Yes," said the rabbi, "that is how it is. Once a rumor, a gossipy story, a secret, leaves your mouth, you do not know where it ends up. It

---

[118] Chabad.org, "A Pillow Full of Feathers" story retold by Shoshannah Brombacher.

flies on the wind, and you can never get it back!"

Gossip and "hearsay" are related to *lashon hara,* and both are to be avoided. Gossip often becomes "catty" and negative about another person. "Hearsay", meaning repeating something that you haven't witnessed firsthand, is a legal term. Hearsay is not admissible evidence in a U.S. court, because it is considered unreliable.

In Jewish folklore *lashon hara* lingers in an invisible world, and it accumulates. It can come back to haunt the person guilty of starting the *lashon hara.*

Not only do you not want to start *lashon hara*, but you should also not act based upon *lashon hara*. You should discourage it.

You certainly don't want *lashon hara* to haunt your business. However, in this era of social media you need to pay attention to customers' "word of mouth", positive and negative.

Jews, like everyone else, look at business reviews, particularly when shopping on-line for major purchases, like selecting a resort or buying a ticket for a play. But we're treading on thin ethical ice here.

It seems okay to read reviews; you are collecting information. You should realize that what you read may be exaggerated and, possibly, may not even be true. Buyer beware!

But, writing a negative review is *lashon hara,* which we shouldn't do. You would be gossiping, at best, and harming a vendor whom you should assume is trying to do their best.

Providing feedback constructively and in private is something different. You would be helping a vendor by giving them honest, constructive feedback. You would be gifting your time to provide information, so that a vendor may improve their product or service.

On occasion, I have written privately to a vendor, for example a hotel, where I did not get good service. But I emphasize that I did this privately. I didn't post my negative comments on their website or a public review site. Rather, I wanted the vendor to know that their service did not meet my expectations, with the hope that they would use the feedback to improve their operations. When I've done this, I always have gotten an apology response from the vendor. Sometimes, though rarely, I have gotten a refund or a coupon to encourage a repeat visit, and while I appreciated the refund that wasn't my main motivation for providing feedback.

Lashon hara also is important in your business with respect to Human Resources. When you are considering hiring someone you generally check out their references. It is okay to ask a prospective employee to give you their references, and it is okay for you to contact them. Keep in mind, though, that the references given to you by a prospective employee are hand-selected, and so are not an unbiased sample. When the shoe is on the other foot, and an ex-employee has given you as a reference, you are not allowed to divulge negative facts about that employee. Today, most large companies HR departments will verify that a person has worked there, but they won't divulge qualitative information about ex-employees.

In any case, shoppers expect to see five-star ratings, or close to it, for any significant purchase, and you can assume that shoppers will check the reviews of your business. Sometimes problems occur, and a customer of yours may have a poor experience at your business. After all, nobody and nothing is perfect. We'll discuss how to remedy or, at least, mitigate such bad experiences in a subsequent chapter.

Strive For Perfection But Expect Reality

> *Tikkun Olam (repair the world) implies that while the world is innately good, its Creator purposely left room for us to improve upon His work.*[119]

Nobody and nothing is perfect.

Prospective customers shouldn't expect perfection all the time, and most rational people understand this.

---

[119] chabad.org, "Ethics and Morality: *Tikkun Olam*"

Smart managements shouldn't expect perfection all the time, either. It's nice to hear positive feedback, but actually it's very helpful, even more helpful, to get negative feedback. We want our businesses to continually improve, and negative feedback helps to pinpoint those areas that need attention.

A smart business response to a negative review, although this is done infrequently, is to offer the person who suffered a bad experience some type of "freebie", some coupon or other way to encourage them to retry your product or service. Basically, say, "Sorry. We'll rectify the problem you experienced right away. Please come back and try us again."

This entails some extra expense for the retailer, and it requires trust that a customer is not just taking advantage of the retailer's good nature.

A few companies have made handling customer complaints into a distinct positive for their business. They take to heart the motto, "The customer is always right". (Think of this as a special case of Leviticus 19:18 "Love thy neighbor as thyself".)

When a business earns a reputation that it sincerely wants every customer to have a good experience, it can turn into a huge positive branding asset. The businesses that do this realize that some customers will take advantage unfairly, but the cost from such customers is outweighed by the gain in sales from their stellar reputations for excellent customer service.

> Nordstrom is an example of "the customer is always right" motto[120]. As the story goes, a woman came into the Customer Service department at Nordstrom to return a set of car tires. The attendant took back the tires. This transaction became famous throughout the company when the CEO called the customer service attendant and congratulated her for allowing the customer to return the tires. Why was this so special? At the time, Nordstrom didn't even sell tires.

---

[120] Ram Charan, called by Fortune magazine "the most influential consultant of all time", used this example in a lecture that I attended years ago. I cannot verify if this story about Nordstrom was true, and I cannot vouch that Nordstrom still practices this motto, at least to the same extent today, although Nordstrom continues to be a very fine and successful retailer.

Many retail and service businesses have complicated processes to deliver their final product, so that the chances are high for something to go wrong. The product must be manufactured perfectly, transported to the retail location without damage, labeled and displayed just right, and the sales representative dealing directly with the customer must be pleasant, prompt, informative, as well as accurate.

Your business also usually must depend upon others that are not within your direct control.

Consider the airline industry in this regard. Just outside the airport a passenger deals with police directing traffic and curbside baggage handlers. In the outside lobby of the airport the passenger waits in line to see a ticket agent and check their baggage, and then waits in another line to go through security. Inside the terminal a passenger may buy food or a magazine and deal with the attendants in those stores. Finally, when the passenger gets onto the airplane, they may interact with another passenger who is not very cooperative in sharing overhead luggage space or cooperating to allow them to get to their window seat. During the flight a baby in a nearby seat may be crying. At the other end of the flight the passenger has to deplane and retrieve their luggage. If their luggage is misplaced, you can bet that the passenger's memory of that flight will be overshadowed by the hassle of reuniting with their luggage. Any of these personal actions can go awry which can make the passenger's trip unpleasant.

Or consider the restaurant business. A lot goes into a customer's experience, from the preparation and presentation of the food to the attractiveness and cleanliness of the establishment. A waiter may make a mistake or not be as attentive as the patron desires. The check might not arrive in a timely manner, or perhaps annoy a patron because the check is brought to the table too soon. The bathroom may not be as clean as it should be, despite a regular periodic cleaning schedule used by the restaurant. Even unusual circumstances, such as a patron tripping on the way to their table or slipping on ice as they leave the restaurant can ruin the patron's whole experience. A patron may get an upset stomach afterwards, possibly through no fault of the restaurant.

Take your own business as an example. Consider all the interactions that a customer has with your business before, during, and after the sale. Consider what could go wrong, and continually improve how you can prevent those mishaps, or at least ameliorate a bad customer experience.

Consider negative occurrences as valuable feedback to plan your next improvements. You are responsible for the overall process, for training, and for motivating your employees.

Don't be too hard on yourself. And be careful to control your frustration and disappointment in how you deal with your employees. Don't get angry with your employee, who may have made a mistake. Rather, turn a mistake into a learning experience.

The Jewish businessperson inherently knows that nothing is perfect. Problems will occur, even though some problems will not be your fault, and certainly not your intention. *God* created the world for people to make it better.

Customers do expect every business to try to be perfect, even though they know that nothing is perfect. Customers will reward you when you acknowledge and try to rectify situations that don't turn out "good enough".

Handle Disagreements Like a Mensch[121]

> *A man should always be soft as a reed and not hard like a cedar.*
>
> \- *Talmud*[122]

Fixing problems that inevitably occur is what *God* intends us to do.

The first step is to acknowledge that a problem has occurred, and this is not so easy.

You've built a good, successful business, and you've invested your time, energy and money into it. You take great pride in what you have accomplished. Now, along comes a customer who doesn't appreciate, or realize, the effort behind the scenes that went into building your business. The customer sees only a result from their own perspective. Perhaps the customer is upset and not so nice in voicing their displeasure. And

---

121 "*Mensch*" is *Yiddish*. A *mensch* is a person who can be relied on to act with honor and integrity. But the *Yiddish* term means more than that; it also suggests someone who is kind and considerate. (The Jewish Chronicle)

122 *Talmud: Taan* 20b

perhaps, your first, honest reaction is that the customer is not being reasonable, that nothing so terrible really happened.

Sometimes your customer will act unreasonably. What if your customer acts like a four-year old?

Recently, my wife and I were babysitting for our four-year old granddaughter, who happened to be sick at the time. Our granddaughter was being unreasonable, crying, not listening to our pleadings to take her medicine. She was four and acting her age. No amount of calm, rational arguing on our part was going to work in that instant. The best way to calm our granddaughter down was to say, "I know. You don't like medicine."

While we, ourselves, were frustrated, the best thing we could do was to diffuse the confrontational situation. You diffuse a confrontation by listening, by being empathetic. Let your granddaughter, er: customer, win a point!

Understand the problem and try to see it from the customer's point-of-view. Clarify, again from the customer's point-of-view, what happened that disappointed the customer.

To help keep your own temper calm, realize, as we have said, that nothing is perfect. The best business process doesn't always produce a perfect result.

A few years back there was a lot of emphasis in business training on quality improvement, and the term "six sigma" was popular in business jargon. Six sigma refers to a statistical test that measures how many defects occur from a business process, with the understanding that all business processes produce some defects. You don't have to understand the statistics, just appreciate that if a process produces less than six sigma defects it is a very good process.

> Early in my career I oversaw compiling the monthly liabilities for insurance claims for my company. Computerization and spreadsheets, at the time, were relatively unsophisticated, and so my job, with my team, involved lots of calculations and assembling of numbers. We were always under time pressure, as we had to get everything together to present to top management.
>
> One time, at the meeting with top management a mistake in our work became apparent. After the meeting my boss pulled me aside and

said, "Joel, this cannot happen again. We cannot make any mistakes!" Naturally, I was upset and frustrated. I accepted the blame for the mistake. But I protested to my boss, "It's impossible to guarantee that we won't ever make another mistake. We compile so many numbers, literally millions of numbers in a short time, that mistakes are inevitable. The process will never be perfect."

My boss let the discussion go at that. He was a good boss and mentor to me.

I cannot say that we didn't ever make a mistake again. But the bar was raised. We had to meet a higher standard for excellence. And we did!

So, don't be overly upset when a business result is not up to your quality standard. It happens. Take it as an opportunity to improve.

After you listen to your unhappy customer, try to offer a solution. You might ask your customer what you can do to make it up to him or her. If you are a restauranteur, for example, your proposed solution might be to void the charge for a particular item. If you offer a service, you might be able to offer your customer a coupon for a return visit or redo the service at no additional cost.

In any case, try to verify with your customer that your proposed solution is acceptable.

Follow-up with your customer to make sure that their return visit or service re-do or whatever is your mutually agreed solution has met your customer's expectations.

You won't win them all. But, some customers, even disappointed customers, should see that you are always trying to make your business better. If you smile and show that you are trying your best, hopefully you won't get yelled at as much.

Who is mighty? He who turns an enemy into his friend.

- *Talmud*[123]

[123] *Talmud: Arn* 23

Put It To Work

Asah (Do)

- Improve your product by using sustainable raw materials as well as making more efficient use of materials.
- Assess how your product impacts other humans and other life forms. Are the impacts positive or at least minimally invasive?
- Consider how your children and your children's children would view your product. What could you do to make them prouder of what you are currently producing?

Bara (Create)

- Make it routine to scan social media and see what your past customers are saying about your business.
- Make it a regular practice and have a standard procedure to thank customers for their patronage, including asking them to tell you of any problems. If a customer is very satisfied with your product or service, ask them for a positive review. If a customer is not satisfied fully, ask them to communicate their issue to you privately so that you may rectify it with them. (It is not lashon hara to say nice things about another person. And it is not lashon hara for a customer to speak directly with you about a problem.)
- Develop procedures to handle poor reviews, whether these reviews are on-line or otherwise communicated to you.
- Continually make improvements in everything that you do in your business.
- Test drive your improvements as much as practical. For example, do a practice run-through with your team. When you are opening a new branch or service try to have a soft opening, a practice run-through for friends and family.
- When a customer has a negative occurrence with your business, acknowledge it, and try to fix it at no additional charge.

- Enjoy solving problems. Try to make this a fun part of your business. Take satisfaction in working hard and doing your best.

- Don't be embarrassed about a mistake. It happens in the best business processes.

- Make correcting your mistakes with your customer a separate business process, itself, with the goal of making the corrective action a positive experience for your customer.

- Your corrective action might be a "money back guarantee", but it's even better to get your customer to agree to a re-do in which you can satisfy their need. Keep in mind that your customer didn't want their money back; they wanted your product or service in the first place.

- Follow up with your customer to verify that they feel satisfied with your product or service.

- Be proud of your attempts to "satisfy every customer". Advertise this.

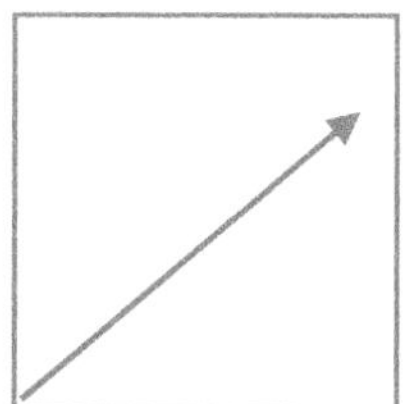

Spread Joy

Smile though your heart is aching
Smile even though it's breaking
When there are clouds in the sky
You'll get by

\- Melody by Charlie Chaplin[124]

Very few people, and perhaps nobody, has a sunny disposition all the time. Not only would that be unrealistic, but it might also even come across as crazy.

But smiles do help. It makes you happier, and you will make people around you happier. In business, people would rather deal with a person who makes them more comfortable. And your team members will work harder and better if they are happy.

[124] First verse of "Smile" made famous by Nat King Cole in 1954. The melody was written by Charlie Chaplin as the theme for his movie "Modern Times". Chaplin apparently was raised by Jewish parents but evaded direct questions about his ethnicity. When asked directly if he was Jewish, Chaplin said, "I am a son of Father Abraham". (Jewish Telegraphic Agency; jta.org)

Business Should Be Fun

What is "fun"? Modern dictionaries define "fun" as something that provides enjoyment, and curiously the word "fun" first appeared in English in the late 1600s. Does that mean that people didn't have fun before 1600. Of course not.

In ancient times people did not have the degree of free time that we enjoy today, and so "having fun" was not one of society's main pursuits[125]. People didn't say, "Let's go have fun." But certainly, people have always gotten enjoyment as an occasional diversion from the serious business of living.

Chasidism, which arose as a spiritual revival movement in Poland in the 18th century, incorporated joyful singing and dancing in their ritual practices. The Jewish Renewal movement, which started in the 20th century and has been characterized as neo-Chasidism, joyfully embraces music, meditation, chant, yoga, and storytelling in their practice of Judaism.

Jack, who was one of my early business mentors, used to say, "Business is fun". He meant that problem solving is fun. And indeed, I enjoyed business problem solving. I enjoyed the creativity and the feeling of satisfaction of having improved the company in some way. I enjoyed doing good.

Jack was not Jewish, and frankly at the time I did not connect solving business problems with Judaism. And obviously, you don't have to be Jewish to be a good businessperson or a good person.

But, as you hopefully have learned throughout this book, Jewish wisdom is quite old, quite solid, and quite useful for solving business problems.

Jewish wisdom teaches us to "go forward". Business, and life, is all about solving problems. And there is great satisfaction, and fun, in doing this well.

Progress happens when we utilize our gifts of observation and ingenuity to innovate. This is what builds businesses. It is what makes business fun and rewarding.

---

[125] Beth Kissileff - forward.com

So, yes. Do good business. Have fun doing so.

Make the Work Environment a Home

We spend a lot of our time at work[126]. The people with whom we work become key relationships in our lives. What we do at work rubs off on our families, and how we handle work is an important example for our kids.

Work styles have caused our work and home environments to become even more blurred. Many people work virtually, or partially virtually. Communication technology facilitates 24/7 contact, so events of the day don't necessarily end when we leave the office or factory or store.

Obviously, work environments need to be useful to facilitate the job at hand. So too, work environments should be be comfortable and welcoming.

Talmud provides additional advice for how to treat people at work. Each of these teachings are examples of Hillel's overriding teaching to treat people as you would like to be treated.

For example, workers must be paid in cash on a timely basis.

> *The wages of a laborer shall not remain with you until morning.*
>
> \- *Leviticus 19:13*

Team members should be encouraged to express their views and ask questions, even when the majority opinion seems to lean differently.

> *The idea of Talmud is that you are allowed to ask questions about anything.*
>
> \- Rabbi Adin Steinsaltz[127]

[126] If we work 8 hours 5 days per week it amounts to about 24% of our time. And many people work "after hours".

[127] Rabbi Steinsaltz is a noted *Talmud* scholar. He is the author of over 60 books on ethics, theology, prayer and mysticism. He is noted for having translated the *Talmud* from ancient Hebrew and Aramaic to Modern Hebrew.

Care for Others

Give me a tenth in order that you will become wealthy.

- Talmud

A common prescription for handling your money is to save, invest, spend, and give. This list implies that giving, or charity, is what is left over from your funds after you spend. But that is not the Jewish way!

Torah commands that we *tithe*, donate ten percent of our earnings. As we have discussed throughout this book, money follows doing good. Part of doing good is to give generously to charity.

You can appreciate essences of a culture by understanding their language. Hebrew has several words for "charity", such as: c*hesed, gemilut hasadim,* and *tzedakah.* But these various Hebrew words have different nuanced meanings[128]. *Chesed* refers to *God*'s kindness to people, and *Torah* commentary remarks that *God*'s *chesed* towards the Hebrews extends even when the Hebrews act disobediently. *Tzedakah* refers to giving money to those less fortunate. *Gemilut hasadim* is often translated as "acts of loving kindness" which includes more than giving money to those less fortunate.

In business we have many occasions to deal with other people: customers, employees, and suppliers. Our interaction often devolves to money, perhaps because money is easy to compare in a business environment. But there are so many opportunities for *gemilut hasadim*, acting kindly to other people beyond satisfying any money obligations. A kindly act demonstrates more than money can accomplish. It shows true caring.

[128] MyJewishLearning.com, "Acts of Loving Kindness" by Rabbi Sara Paasche-Orlow

Give Thanks

> *All man's possession are but a loan from the Creator of the Universe, to Whom belong the earth and the fullness thereof, and by his charity he merely secures a more equitable distribution of God's gifts to mankind.*
>
> \- Abraham Cohen[129]

We started this book with "Who's the Boss?", and throughout the book we discussed many business topics that shared the common theme expressed in the quote above.

Jewish wisdom is very rich (pun intended). Successful businesspeople, Jews and non-Jews, should give thanks to *God*, who they know deep down, is the original Creator.

Modern progressive Jews who are not as observant of Jewish traditions know that their business success is not based solely on their own effort. They know that their own intelligence is inherited and trained. They know that their schooling and other opportunities are privileges. They know that success can be transitory. They want to pass along worthy values to their children, and not just money.

Doing Good is the real purpose of business. Being creative and building value in business is a privilege.

Be thankful.

Put It To Work

Asah (Do)

- Enjoy your work. Be enthused and satisfied by your hard work to make things better.
- Smile! Smiles and a positive attitude are contagious. Pass it on.

[129] Abraham Cohen, Everyman's Talmud: The Major Teachings of the Rabbinic Sages, Schocken, February 1995

- Listen open-mindedly to the views of your employees.
- Explain key decisions that you make to managers that report to you. When practical seek input to decisions beforehand.
- Give ample time to your family, away from work.
- Take your kids to work sometimes, if at all practical.
- Celebrate your work victories with your spouse and kids.

Bara (Create)

- Teach your children by providing them with an allowance. Permit them freedom to choose how they spend it.
- Be thankful for your gifts of intelligence and freedom.
- Make giving a priority. Demonstrate your caring by doing kind acts for others. Give to good causes.
- Bring spirituality into your business life.
- Observe how alike are all peoples in their search for peace, prosperity and happiness.

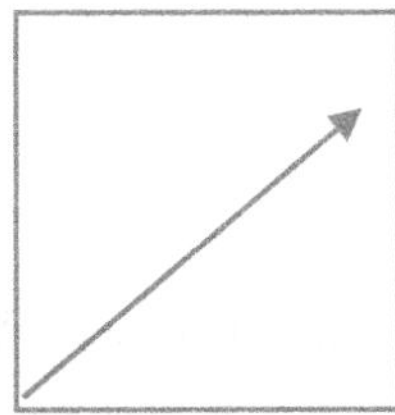

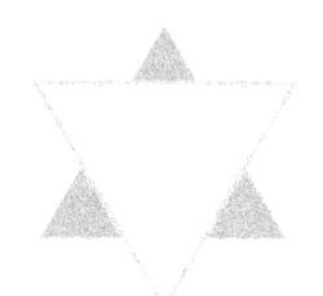

Be A Jewish (or Non-Jewish) Star

Anyone can talk with God.

- Rabbi Nachman, (1772-1810) a great *Chassidic* master

Judaism encourages everyone to have a personal relationship with *God.*

Rabbi Nachman encouraged his followers to talk to *God* every day and to do so in their native language. He recommended, "Talk about anything: complaints, efforts for self-improvement, the state of the world, anything."[130]

His teachings were intended to break down barriers between one's secular life and spiritual life. Excellent advice! In America, where most of us enjoy freedoms and excellent secular education, we tend to separate our religious practices from our everyday life. Because we respect so much the separation of church and State, we miss the synergies.

Throughout this book we've discussed how to increase your chances for success in life and business? In the business world we tend to call these "best practices". Hopefully, we've also shown how founded these business recommendations are in age-old Jewish wisdom.

Enhance your life, with your family and friends and in your business, by bringing these teachings together. Break down barriers between your secular and spiritual thinking. Allow spiritualism into your everyday life.

You'll be amazed and inspired by the synergies.

[130] MyJewishLearning.org "How to Talk to God" by Rabbi David Jaffe

Different Pathways to Knowledge

Jewish traditions are based upon thousands of years of observed practices that enhance life. Science is another way of observing nature to explain life.

There is no dichotomy between these pathways to knowledge, except the artificial walls that we've let develop. Each path of study has its own rules and even its own biases. But, the goals are the same, to understand life and make it better.

Jewish tradition is very old, and ancient ways of thinking naturally were stated in the language and understanding of the times. Jewish tradition developed to guide human behavior in healthy ways. At the time that many Jewish traditions were developed the society was mostly agrarian. No surprise, then, that Jewish society was very aware of nature's impacts on human life, and a deep respect for nature is inherent in much of Jewish tradition.

Jewish traditions have evolved through the ages, and today there is a range of varying practices. Orthodox practices remain closer to ancient practices, while Reform and other congregations have tried to modify traditional practices considering contemporary influences. Nevertheless, the underlying principles are the same.

Science, similarly, is based upon keen observation of nature. Scientists are keenly aware of what they do not know.

> *To raise new questions, new possibilities, to regard old problems from a new angle, requires creative imagination and marks real advance in science.*
>
> \- Einstein

Find answers through the lens of both science and Jewish spirituality. Both lead to knowledge and more learning.

Every answer can result in a new question.

- *Yiddish* saying

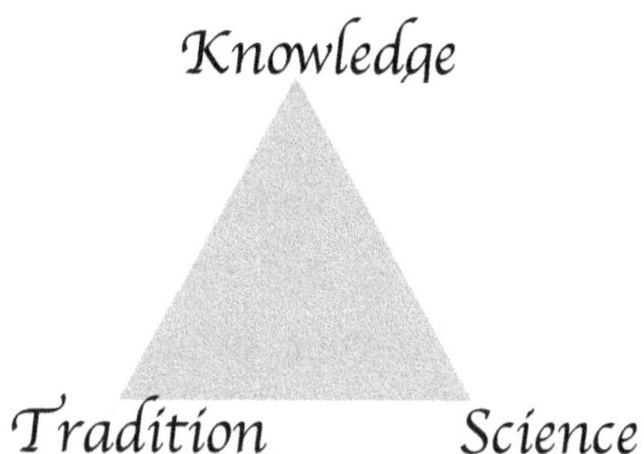

Practice What You Preach

Researching for this book I was struck by the marvelously robust Jewish influences throughout history and extending into modern times. Jewish thinkers, artists, scientists, and business leaders since ancient times have advanced our ways of understanding our world.

Our ancient rabbis interpreted *Torah* and developed a code of conduct that is at the heart of Judaism. This knowledge synthesized natural law with human behavior norms. The *Talmud* was developed, and among other things served as the governing knowledge for Jewish society for centuries.

In the Middle Ages *Kabbalah* was developed, spawning another surge in spiritual studies. The *Chassidic* movement that emerged still energizes Jews around the world.

In relatively modern times Jews have been particularly exemplary in advancing knowledge in medicine and the sciences as well as popular culture. The songs, humor, and literature, some of which is quoted in this book, reflect insightful knowledge that updates ancient Jewish knowledge for a modern context.

In business we call the things that we should do "best practices". Each of these best practices can be linked to wisdom cultivated in the Jewish traditions.

Any one of these best practices, if you implement them, would benefit your career and your business. Putting many of these best practices to use would very significantly increase your chances for success.

The key, though, is doing them. Much as you may nod your head in agreement that these practices make sense, it takes continuous intent to instill these best practices as good habits. Consequently, practical to-do steps (*asah*) are provided at the end of each chapter, and creative steps (*bara*) are listed for you to think about and apply to your business situations.

Share these business lessons with your business teammates. Doing them together will enhance your team's success and make it more likely that these good practices will be continued.

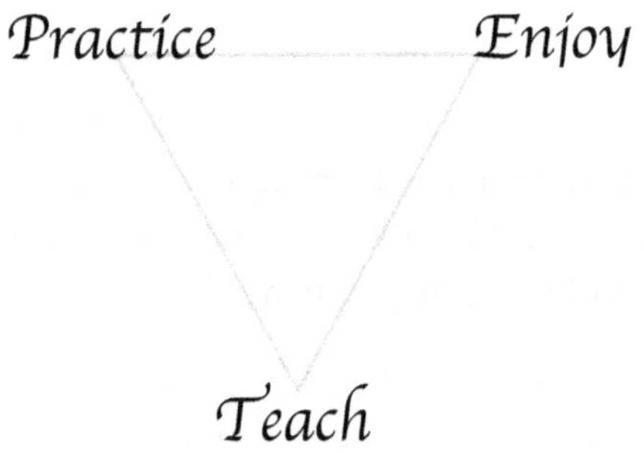

Practice Enjoy

Teach

Find Spirituality in Everything

Doing and creating based upon Jewish wisdom obviously applies not only to your business. Doing these things will help make your family and community life more enjoyable too. You will be more successful in life.

Discuss this wisdom and practice employing these suggestions with your spouse. Teach them to your children. The success will spread. You'll get lots of *nachas,* joy.

This wisdom is not just for Jews; anyone can benefit. Rephrase these lessons in language that is comfortable in your own tradition. But practice this wisdom and you will see the twinkle in the Jewish star.

Bibliography

Books

Kai Bird and Martin Sherwin, American Prometheus: The Triumph and Tragedy of J. Robert Oppenheimer, Atlantic Books, January 2009

Martin Buber, I and Thou, 1923

Maristella Botticini and Zvi Eckstein, The Chosen Few: How Education Shaped Jewish History, 70-1492, Princeton, 2012

Thomas Cahill, The Gifts of the Jews, Anchor, 1999

Abraham Cohen, Everyman's Talmud: The Major Teachings of the Rabbinic Sages, Schocken, 1995

Edwin Dolan, TANSTAAFL, 1971

Viktor Frankl, Man's Search of Meaning, 1946

Neal Gabler, An Empire of Their Own: How the Jews Invented Hollywood, Random House, 1998

Abraham Joshua Heschel, God in Search of Man; A Philosophy of Judaism, Harper and Row, January 1966

Harold Kushner, When Bad Things Happen to Good People, Avon, January 1, 1983

Dr. Burton Malkiel, A Random Walk Down Wall Street, 1973

Daniel Matt, PhD , God and the Big Bang: Discovering Harmony Between Science and Spirituality, Jewish Lights Publishing, April 2016

Chaim Potok, Wanderings, Knopf, 1978

Daniel Schulman, The Money Kings, Knopf, 2023

Michael Shevack, The Six Fix, Spiritual Healthcare for a Stronger America, Enlightened Religion Press, 2023

Jeremy Siegel, Stocks for the Long Run, McGraw Hill, October 2022

Max Weber; Peter R. Baehr; Gordon C. Wells, The Protestant Ethic and the "Spirit" of Capitalism, Penguin Twentieth Century Classics, 2002

Websites

Biblestudytools.com/rsv

Chabad.org

ExploringJudaism.org

MyJewishLearning.org

ReformJudaism.org

Sefaria.org

Yiddishwit.com/List

About the Author

Joel has had a successful career in management consulting and senior corporate roles. He is an expert in finance and in strategic and marketing planning. He has been the CFO of several companies.

As a consultant Joel specialized in helping insurance companies throughout the United States to improve. Often this involved streamlining their products, reorganizing their operations, developing management information systems and process improvements.

As a company executive, Joel's forte was bridging the financial function with other departments for cross-functional cooperation and improvement.

Joel is a former President of Temple Judea of Bucks County, a Reform synagogue, where he was instrumental in engineering and leading a turnaround in that organization. As part of this experience and continuing since, Joel became keenly interested in Judaism and the synergies between business theory and Jewish philosophy.

Joel graduated from Drexel University with a degree in mathematics. He has an MBA from Wharton. He is a retired member of the Casualty Actuarial Society and American Academy of Actuaries. He also is an Enterprise Risk Analyst.

He resides in New Hope, Pennsylvania with his wife Carol. Their children and grandchildren live in New Jersey. Joel is an avid, amateur guitarist and enjoys hiking and swimming.

www.ingramcontent.com/pod-product-compliance
Lightning Source LLC
LaVergne TN
LVHW010544160826
845677LV00013B/2995

* 9 7 9 8 9 8 7 9 5 0 2 7 2 *